Stone Roses

"*Talking*"

OMNIBUS PRESS

STONE ROSES *Talking*

Copyright © 2003 Omnibus Press
(A Division of Music Sales Limited)

Cover & Book designed by Fresh Lemon.
Picture research by Sarah Bacon.

ISBN: 0.7119. 9890.6
Order No: OP 49577

Exclusive Distributors
Music Sales Limited, 8/9 Frith Street, London W1D 3JB, UK.

Music Sales Corporation,
257 Park Avenue South, New York, NY 10010, USA.

Macmillan Distribution Services,
53 Park West Drive, Derrimut, Vic 3030, Australia.

To the Music Trade only:
Music Sales Limited, 8/9 Frith Street, London W1D 3JB, UK.

Photo credits:
Front Cover: Kevin Cummins / Retna UK; Back cover: LFI
Matt Anker / Retna: 100, 110 (main pic); Steve Double / Retna: 120;
Chris Floyd / Camera Press: 101; Ross Gilmore / Redferns: 97;
Martyn Goodacre / Retna: 3, 43, 109 (main pic); LFI: 4, 7, 9, 14, 18, 19,
20, 21, 22, 25, 27, 30, 31, 36, 39, 50, 55, 57, 64 (below), 67, 69, 70 (main pic),
77 (main pic), 80, 81, 82 (main pic), 83, 88 (main pic), 90, 91, 92, 93,
95 (main pic), 98 (main pic), 102, 103, 105, 106, 114 (main pic), 115,
122 (main pics), 123, 124, 127, 128; Michel Linssen / Redferns: 84;
Hayley Madden / Redferns: 73; Anthony Pidgeon / Retna: 117;
Brian Rasic / Rex Features: 79, 94, 105 (main pic); Johnny Rosza / Retna: 74;
Roger Sargent / Rex Features: 108; Ed Sirrs / Retna: 40, 118; Paul Slattery: 10, 12,
13, 17, 23, 25 (main pic), 26, 28, 30, 32, 33, 34, 35, 42, 45, 46, 47, 48, 49,
51, 52, 55 (main pic), 60, 63, 65, 69 (main pic), 70, 76, 77, 78, 86, 88, 89, 109,
110, 113, 119, 122, 125, 126 (main pic); Jon Super / Redferns: 112;
Ian Tilton / Retna: 39 (main pic), 58, 64 (top); Ian Tilton / SIN: 11, 15, 60, 66
Colour Picture Section Credits: Stephen Butler / Rex Features: 7, Chris Clunn / Retna: 3, 8;
LFI: 2, 4; Ebet Roberts / Redferns: 5; Johnny Rosza / Retna: 1; Simon Taylor / SIN: 6

Every effort has been made to trace the copyright holders
of the photographs in this book but one or two were unreachable.
We would be grateful if the photographers concerned would contact us.

Printed by Caligraving Ltd, Thetford, Norfolk.

A catalogue record for this book is available from the British Library.

Visit Omnibus Press on the web at www.omnibuspress.com

ACKNOWLEDGEMENTS
The author would like to thank Nigel Cross of NWC Productions
for his vital research assistance.

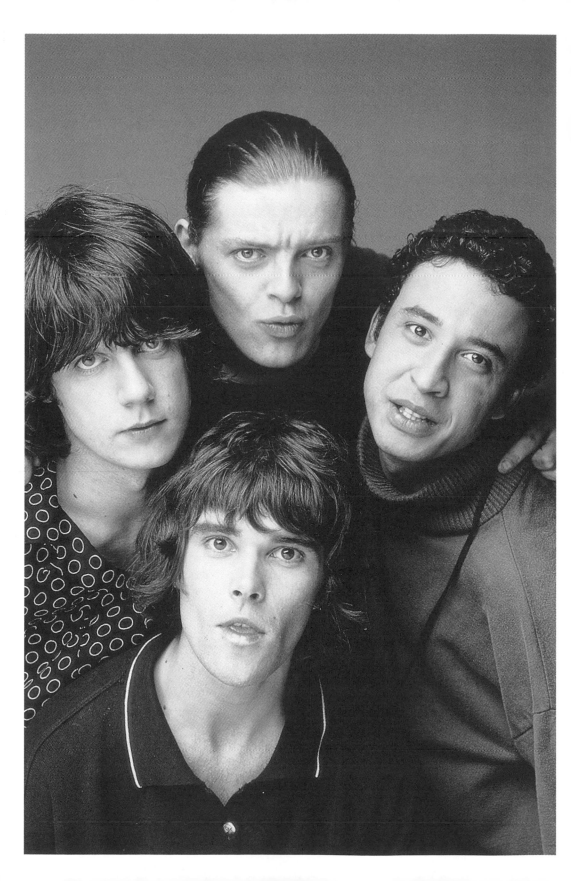

CONTENTS

 **STONE ROSES** *Talking*

There's a generation out there that will tell you The Stone Roses saved rock, and they'd have a case. The music scene by the mid-1980s in the UK was stagnant; almost but not quite dead on its feet. The Smiths might've been a great pop band but they never rocked – they weren't allowed to. Most self-respecting cool kids were fully signed-up members of the rave culture by then anyway. Yet when the Roses' eponymous debut album set the charts ablaze in the summer of 1989, rock rose from the grave. I am the resurrection, indeed.

From humble beginnings in Chorlton, Manchester, through scooter gangs and early combos such as The Patrol, childhood friends Ian Brown and John Squire slowly found their feet.

Introduction

It took their new band, The Stone Roses, some time but eventually they fashioned a unique sound and an equally unique image that oozed an attitude and integrity not witnessed since punk's heyday – all for one and one for all became their motto. Drummer Alan 'Reni' Wren was an early find though, as with most bands, additional members - namely second guitarist Andy Couzens and bassist Pete Garner – dropped out along the way (though fifth member and stage dancer, 'Cressa', survived.) With the arrival of bassist Gary 'Mani' Mounfield in 1987, the Roses finally settled on their classic line up and sound, becoming a true rock 'n' roll four piece in the grand tradition of The Beatles, The Who and The Clash.

Along with The Happy Mondays, the Roses' music became the soundtrack of its time. They bust the indie scene wide open and put 'Madchester' on the rock 'n' roll map. The sky seemed the proverbial limit. The band's eponymous first album, with its classic Jackson Pollock-style sleeve designed by Squire, brought in freshness, passion and excitement with its funky rhythms and cascading, psych-like guitars. Drawing heavily on rock classicism, anthems like 'Waterfall' caught the imagination of both press and public. Already huge in their native North, the Roses looked like they were about to take the world by storm. Magnificent pioneering singles followed, like 'Fool's Gold',

one of the first records to successfully marry Acid House with rock 'n' roll. The UK went mad for them – triumphant live shows at the Empress Ballroom, Blackpool and Spike Island were events that have become part of English rock folklore.

The Roses were the stuff of legend; becoming one of the most controversial bands since The Sex Pistols. One story has it that the original title of the band's stunning debut LP was to be called *Bring Me The Head Of James Anderton On A Plate*, a reference to the God-fearing, right-wing chief constable of Manchester. Another anecdote has Ian Brown taking £100,000 in cash out of the bank when the hefty advance from Geffen Records came through and distributed it to the poor and needy of Manchester. During their first wave of success, the band faced criminal damage charges for spray painting Paul Birch, the man behind the FM-Revolver label, who reissued 'Sally Cinnamon' with a promotional video they disapproved of. The band later became embroiled in a series of lawsuits with both the Silvertone record label and former manager Gareth Evans.

Sadly, it was to be a slow decline from the heady heights of '89. The band took an unprecedented five years to release the follow-up to that hugely influential debut, plagued by the court cases, family responsibilities and personal problems –and, when *Second Coming* appeared, it was seen by many as an anti-climax. Full of bluesy riffs and virtuoso guitar playing that drew heavily on the late Sixties school of heavy rock, it failed to excite those who'd loved the melodic lightness of its predecessor, which called to mind the psychedelia of The Beatles, The Byrds and "paisley underground" bands from the mid-Eighties like The 3 O'Clock and The Rain Parade. The dance rhythms were conspicuous by their absence.

This was an album made by an older, wiser, and more cynical Roses. John Squire had got his mojo working, summoning up the voodoo blues power of the Jimi Hendrix Experience, the Jeff Beck Group, and Led Zeppelin. Back in 1994 there was no journalist brave enough to applaud this startling new direction – Robert Plant appearing on a Primal Scream album was way down the line – and it's ironic that nobody has subsequently drawn a direct correlation between *Second Coming* and the current wave of critically-acclaimed blues-rockers like The White Stripes and Kings Of Leon.

INTRODUCTION

It was a shame that there was little input from Ian Brown compared to the first album, as apparently his vocals weren't strong enough to carry some of the heavier numbers. In retrospect, a great record.

Within months of its release, the writing was on the wall. Firstly, drummer Reni followed by guitarist Squire unexpectedly quit. Remaining members Brown and Mani recruited drummer Robbie Maddix and keyboardist Nigel Ippinson, with guitarist Aziz Ibrahim in place of Squire. This latter line-up met their Waterloo at the Reading Festival in August 1996, turning in a lacklustre set. It was to be their ignominious farewell. At the same time, another Manchester guitar band rose phoenix-like from the Roses' ashes. Oasis ushered in the Britpop era, with brothers Noel and Liam Gallagher making no secret of their debt to the Roses.

Since the split, the ex-Roses have enjoyed varying fortunes – Squire led The Seahorses and released a fine folksy solo album. Reni fronted his own band The Rub, as singer/guitarist, while Mani, as well as becoming the powerhouse bass player in Primal Scream, occasionally performs with a Roses tribute band, The Complete Stone Roses. Ian Brown has remained consistently controversial. A spell in prison for an alleged air-rage offence failed to halt a series of excellent solo records such as *Unfinished Monkey Business* and *Music From The Spheres*, as well as collaborations with dance acts like UNKLE.

Various ex-members, especially Mani, have kept the door open as to a possible re-union. The bad blood between Brown and Squire remains an obstacle, though a wonderful, possibly apocryphal, story has it that while Brown was doing his time in Strangeways prison in 1998, Squire sent him a note and a box of Maltesers, the gift he'd given Ian every Christmas since they were kids. An olive branch of sorts...

Most will argue that the parts have never equalled the sum, and the biggest question on most Roses fans' minds still remains: Will There Be A Second Coming?

STONE ROSES *Talking*

Growing Up

“My first memory is being about five, at school, and being asked to give out the school milk. And I refused to do it. I said 'No – just put the milk crate on the desk. Everybody can get their own.' I think it was the first day or something, but I thought that if I did it then, I'd have to do it every day. Huh, huh… in the end, that's what they did – they put the milk on the desk and everyone 'ad to come and get their own. Yeah I changed the system! From the start, you 'ave to. Heh heh heh!” **IAN (1990)**

“I sent [*Blue Peter*] a picture of me guinea pig having a bath in the kitchen bowl. I got a *Blue Peter* badge and a signed letter from Biddy Baxter, 'cos it went up on the pictures-of-your-pets board.” JOHN (1995)

“I didn't hear a bad song until I left home.”

JOHN ON HIS UPBRINGING (1989)

“My dad worked at GEC in Trafford Park as an electrical engineer and my mum worked in a chemist, travel agents, fancy goods shop, pub… [my dad] gives me things he's made, radios and stuff, and he pops the circuit diagram in the box just in case I need it… I think he does harbour some sort of notion that I'll get into it one day. But they knocked his factory down so I'm glad I didn't follow him. I'm sure he wouldn't have recommended it, either. He worked there from age 14 to 65 and when he left he had the option of a carriage clock or two hundred quid. Bunch of cunts.”

JOHN (2002)

“They didn't go out drinking, they gave us everything, every Christmas was happy. All they ever gave me was love.” **IAN ON HIS PARENTS (2002)**

10

"I had an uncle who tried to get me into Led Zeppelin." IAN (1989)

"Seeing The Clash at Manchester Apollo in 1977, the 'Complete Control Tour' I think it was called. It was the first gig I'd been to. I'd been listening to the band's music for about a year [*sic*] and was obsessed with them and it was the first time I'd seen them in the flesh. It was just the most exciting thing I'd ever experienced, being right down front and being thrown over the barrier into the pit and being taken out by the side and being put back again. I can remember feeling at the time, 'This is where I want to be,' but I figured it would be more comfortable on the other side of the fence." **JOHN (2003)**

"'God Save The Queen' really made me want to start learning to play the guitar. I was already into The Clash when I heard that. My dad took the transformer off my train set. It had a knob on it that controlled the acceleration. He rigged it up so that it controlled the speed on the record deck. I used to just tune the guitar down and pick things out..."

JOHN (2002)

GROWING UP

"We lived in the same street in Chorlton. I met Ian when we were four or five in a sand pit. I was a bit dubious about him, because the lad he was playing with was bollock naked!" JOHN (1989)

"Just sort of started listening to records me mam played at home, Elvis, the Stones, y'know..." IAN (1989)

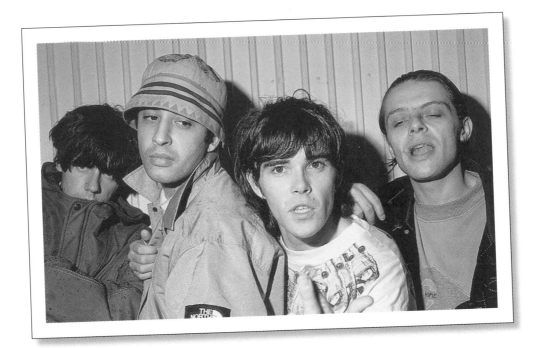

"No-one knows where I was born. Me mum was movin' about a lot at the time." RENI (1990)

"At the time, even though you were 13, you could see the difference between a band like the Sex Pistols and anything else because they were *real*. They weren't like pop stars – 'let's have an autograph.' You thought, 'he's just a lad like me'. It was really exciting when that happened. Everyone was into it mainly due to the Bill Grundy show, I think. We all thought it was excellent - someone swearing on the telly at tea time and hardly any of us had seen the show so there was that added bit of mystery to it."

IAN (1990)

❝I knew, all the time at school, I didn't want a proper job. I didn't want something that would take my brain and my spirit away, working eight hours a day. I didn't always think, 'I want to be in a group'. I didn't know what I wanted to do. Still don't.❞ IAN (1989)

❝The first thing I did was scrub pots! Been left school two days and I'm in this big oven in a hotel with the chef kicking me. That's when I realised I didn't want a job. I stood it about three weeks. Since then I've done bits and pieces. Worked in an office, worked on a building site, worked washing caravans. On the dole, mostly...❞ IAN (1989)

❝I've had loads of crap jobs. I worked at Safeways for a bit, stacking shelves. I worked in a pub, an electronics firm, sweeping up. Reni did some sign-writing, Ian worked in a hotel, Mani worked in an abattoir. I don't like work. I wouldn't mind being a travelling painter, a potter or a bricklayer, though.❞ JOHN (1989)

❝I wasn't an illustrator, I was in the Mud Pie Department, modelling. Good fun...❞

JOHN TALKING ABOUT HIS JOB AT
ANIMATORS COSGROVE HALL (1989)

❝I've always been on the move. When I lived in Sale, I never hung about there. I hung about with lads all over the city. I've been to every seaside town in England and to most cities before we toured. I've been to most of Europe just moving about. It's what I'm into doing.❞

IAN (1989)

GROWING UP

Early Blooms: The Formative Years

66 We were dead tight – as friends, players, *everything*. The sense of belief in ourselves that we had could never be shaken. 99 IAN (2002)

66 As a group we were inseparable. We used to have a thing called the Egg. Us four were inside it, with everyone else pecking away at the shell trying to get in at us. We'd have our own language. It was like a cross between Unwinese and Esperanto. 99 MANI (2002)

66 When I was 17, I used to put a Northern Soul club on with my mate in Salford at The Black Lion in Blackfriars Street. We used to hire a room for £15 and all our mates would come down. We used to build scooters to go to the All-Nighters – just to get girls, really. 99
IAN (2002)

66 I met John at the Northern Soul room at Pips. I met Ian in the fight against fascism – through my little gang of scooter boys in North Manchester. We were having trouble with this gang of local skinheads. The word went out to Ian's South Manchester crew, who came over. We joined forces and hospitalised them. I remember vividly meeting Ian and

thinking, 'that kid looks like Galen off *Planet Of The Apes*.' He always had that striking simian thing. And I liked him from day one because he looked like my favourite telly programme. Even now, his number in my book is under 'King Monkey'.** MANI (2002)

I bumped into Reni at Belle Vue fair years ago. He was rampaging around with a gang of thugs and they bullied me into giving them 10p.

IAN (1988)

When I went to audition for this lot, I thought they were a horrible racket, but I was struck by their commitment. The whole group were such an oddball collection of long-hairs, scruffs and smoothies that I just had to join. RENI (1988)

I've done lots of illegal things, tons, loads... I remember once driving me girlfriend's car and I wasn't insured or taxed or 'ad a license or anything. And I ran into the back of this woman right in the middle of Rusholme. So I just 'ad to leave the car with the doors open, right in the middle of the road in the middle of the rush hour and walk off like I'm Clint Eastwood. Heh heh! The traffic was stopped for miles! RENI (1990)

Yeah, I was dead jealous of the original Roses bassist but... I always knew I was the main man for the job. And you know, I believe heavily in fate and the day it 'appened I was walkin' on me lunch break from work and they were lookin' for a new bass player. We 'adn't seen each other for about eight months and we just bumped into each other on Oxford Road. And I just said, 'Alright, I'll give up me job and do it'. Well weird. Written in the stars, definitely. MANI (1990)

EARLY BLOOMS

❝I knew Ian and John already. We were ex-punks kicking about on the Manchester scooter scene, digging Motown and Northern Soul. I'd been in a band with John – the Waterfront with Andy Couzens and Chris Goodwin – so he knew I was capable. I found out that the Roses needed a new bass player through my brother Greg. I got hold of Squire's number and called him up. 'The job's mine,' I said. Simple as that. They were sick of auditioning bassists and John sounded relieved. 'We should have come to you first,' he said.❞

MANI (2001)

❝There's this story of me girl's 21st party in Hulme, and Geno Washington ending up there after he'd played some cabaret club in Salford that night. He did say to me, 'You're a star. You should be a singer.' I swear I'd never thought about it before then. But that got me thinking about singing seriously. At the same time John had really got into playing guitar. He asked me, 'Do you fancy singing?' At first I thought, this is a poncey sort of thing to be. But John kept getting better and this guy Geno was still in my head. I thought, perhaps he really has seen something in me – something I can't see. So, in 1985, we tried it out and it started to make sense.❞ IAN (2002)

❝The name was a contradiction – something hard and something pretty, something noisy but tuneful.❞ **JOHN ON THE BAND'S NAME (1988)**

❝It was meant to be happy, not Goth-y.❞ IAN ON THE BAND'S NAME (1988)

❝Wild sounds with attractive melodies. We chose the name, The Stone Roses because it reflects this contradiction.❞ **JOHN (1999)**

❝We once wanted to call ourselves The Angry Young Teddy Bears. Someone once wrote that we were Teddy Bears capable of a nasty bite.❞ IAN (1989)

❝Our sound's really rough and powerful.❞ **ANDY COUZENS (1985)**

STONE ROSES *Talking*

❝It's like being hit by a ton of bricks, but there's always a tune.❞

IAN (1985)

❝We used to have a bassist who had hair down to his hips. We were loud, noisy, tuneless, big-mouthed, brash and bratty but *never* dodgy.❞ **IAN (1989)**

❝We were terrible at the start. We couldn't write even a melody line, the sound was just rubbish... even now I blush to think of it.❞ IAN (1989)

❝Steve was and is the entertainment's manager and style guru. Never officially on the payroll but never short of money either. He did a couple of tours with The High in the same capacity.❞

ANDY COUZENS ON THE ROSES' OCCASIONAL DANCER STEVE CRESSER (2001)

"It takes effort to sound effortless. Like it's hard work not working. Being on the dole takes great endurance, 'cos you have to use your imagination otherwise you'll stagnate." IAN (1989)

"None of us has ever considered this band a hobby. We got together with the deliberate intention of composing classic songs and that's just about what we've done." **JOHN (1987)**

"The crucial strengths of this band are our songwriting abilities and our collective presence on stage. That's why we appeal to so many people: we're original, commercial and inspirational at the same time." JOHN (1987)

"There just wasn't anything about when we started in the early 1980s. It was really shit then, music, wasn't it? So we thought we'd do it ourselves. John started getting good on guitar, but he couldn't sing. I was a mate and I could sing so I did. Realised we needed a good drummer. Got one. Played a few gigs, made a few bad records, realised that we had to learn how to make songs rather than just noises. Started writing songs. And here we are."

IAN (1990)

"People just had this preconceived idea that we were hooligans all the time, so we were blamed for the graffiti thing. I don't know why everyone got so upset. It was just some mates. We didn't know about it until afterwards. We know who did it but we're not gonna tell."

IAN ON THE GRAFFITI CAMPAIGN AROUND MANCHESTER IN THE MID-EIGHTIES (1990)

"The argument actually happened in 1985 just prior to the release of 'So Young' and was presented as a *fait accompli*. Reni and I both walked out but were persuaded to return on the promise that it was just an image thing, nothing had changed and all proceeds would be split equally. It took me a year to realise that these people who had been my closest friends and who I trusted implicitly were in fact lying. So I left." **ANDY COUZENS ON THE SONGWRITING CREDITS ARGUMENT THAT LED TO HIS DEPARTURE FROM THE BAND (2002)**

EARLY BLOOMS

Albums & Singles

"You can make yourself everlasting by making records, you can leave a document." **IAN (1988)**

So Young b/w Tell Me (debut single)

"Yeah, because it was so well-known in Manchester, it's become an albatross and we've got to shake it off." **IAN (1988)**

"Too much enthusiasm and not enough thought went into that record. They weren't really songs, just a sound. We've learned how to write now." IAN (1988)

"… [sounds] like four lads trying to get out of Manchester."

IAN (CIRCA 1989)

"Dreadful, angst-ridden rock." IAN (1990)

"It wasn't awful, it was explosive. Martin Hannett's first remix of that track was the most extreme thing I've ever heard… so loud it made Reni's nose explode!" **IAN (2000)**

Sally Cinnamon

❝'Sally' was a sort of semi-conscious effort to shake off 'So Young', which unfortunately sounds quite Goth-y and was big in the Ritz. People actually thought we were Goths and were pissed off that we had short hair.❞ **IAN (1988)**

Elephant Stone

❝He [producer Peter Hook] just liked our song I think. We had rated New Order's dance tunes. When 'Elephant Stone' was ready to record, we started to look for a good producer for a dance record then we hit on his name.❞ **IAN (1989)**

❝**It's our third single but we're all looking on it as a debut as it's the first one we all feel really behind.**❞ IAN (1988)

❝It's about a girl... who I don't see any more.❞ **JOHN (1988)**

Made Of Stone

❝It's about making a wish and watching it happen. Like scoring a goal in a Cup Final... on a Harley Electroglide... dressed as Spiderman.❞ **JOHN (1989)**

Guernica

"We go to Manchester Airport in the summer and watch
the planes land and take off. Your eardrums feel like they're
shredding with the volume of the engines. And the fire coming out
the back. It's an awesome sight, 30 feet from a plane. We want to
get that sound on to record – bits of 'Guernica' sound like planes,
but it's just 'Made Of Stone' backwards with forward vocals.
I'd love to have done it as an A-side." IAN (1989)

Stone Roses (album)

"That LP sold something like three and a half million and I've never
seen a fucking penny. But in the first place it was never about
money. Still money fucked us up in the end. The best bands – Big
Star, Love, the MC5 – never concern themselves with those things.
But they never get paid either." MANI (2002)

**"The first producer we really wanted was DJ Pierre, who did acid
house records at Phuture. Roddy McKenna at Zomba tracked
him down to some tower block in Chicago. I was on the phone to
this kid for about an hour, telling him why we loved his records.
He seemed to us to be the boy to do it. But he had three months'
work on so he couldn't."** IAN (2002)

"We always listened to psychedelia. That's why John Leckie was
right for the first LP. I'd got those great spoof psychedelic LPs by
The Dukes of Stratosphear [XTC] which he produced." MANI (2002)

**"I thought it could have been a lot better, and I wish we could
have done more with it, but, at the end of the day, we decided
to let it go. The next one will be even better though! We know a
lot more now; we've learnt how to play our instruments better."**

IAN (1990)

66 I don't think it matters whether it's a debut album or not. We achieved what we wanted to achieve, we still haven't recorded the ultimate album but it was a good start. 99 IAN (1989)

66 **If we'd had more experience, the first LP would sound more like 'Fools Gold' than it does. 'Cos we see all those songs as being dance tracks. When we play them live, everyone is dancing to them. Not just bobbing up and down, proper *dancing*. The production of the LP isn't really where we are at. But the songs are strong so they came through.** 99 IAN (1989)

66 We had beginnings and endings worked out for all the songs, everything was worked out. 'Sugar Spun Sister', for example, had to finish on a particular chord. We were absolute about how that should be – so well prepared. The Stone Roses *never* winged it. We never had to. 99 IAN (2002)

66 **Well the first album was great fun... we did it in four sessions, in Battery in Willesden, a couple in Konk in Crouch End, then in Rockfield, and Abbey Road. Obviously John Leckie was great to work with, so it was fantastic.** 99 IAN (1998)

66 Everything on that first Roses album was written with acoustic guitar and a Bontempi organ. 99 IAN (1998)

66 **It's timeless. It still sounds fresh. I think if it came out this week it would still make an impact. I remember finally finishing the LP and John Leckie saying to us, 'You're going to do really well, you know'. And we just said, 'Yeah we know'. And we did. We just felt it. He was a bit taken aback by our confidence. But we did know we were good.** 99 IAN (2002)

66 I think it was mainly the production. We saw there being a huge gulf between the live sound of The Stone Roses and that first album. It was mostly recorded on an SSL desk, and it just didn't sound fat or hard enough. From a guitar point of view I see my approach as the main failing. I completely deconstructed what

I played live and re-wrote everything for the studio. That just seems a bit simple, and the switch from chordal to solo stuff just doesn't seem to work. **"**The album just doesn't have the same stamp of a real guitar player to me, apart from a couple of the solos. It sounds like a two guitar band, which we weren't. But I do like the guitar playing on 'Bye Bye Badman.' I worked through the guitar parts for that in this little breeze-blocked room at the back of the studio where all the air-conditioning and mains switches were.**"** JOHN (1997)

"I've got tapes of the first LP where it's as heavy as *Second Coming*. On the album it was all mixed down, but originally the bass 'n' drums were really, really heavy." IAN (1995)

"The low point of that album? I'd have done less overdubs, had stronger main guitar parts.**"** JOHN (1997)

I Am The Resurrection

"That's to do with church publicity. There was a big church in town that had a big yellow day-glo sign up with that line on it.**"**

JOHN (1989)

"I saw a poster with the words that had been written with fluorescent paint, that was put on the door of a church and it impressed me. So this lyric is about anti-Christianity. If people have a normal brain, they should find out how false this statement is. But sometimes people need mental support even though they understand

the real meaning. Very sad or ironic, the Church is making money... the Roman Catholic Church is the richest religious organisation in the world, everyone must know that. "" IAN (1989)

""It was me who coaxed them to do that ending on 'Resurrection.' Only prog rock groups and players up their own arses did 10-minute guitar solos. But I kept saying to them 'Look, you're great. Let's do a 10-minute song where you're just playing and playing and playing.' For two days I watched them work out the ending to that song. It was just fantastic and it still sounds amazing.**"" IAN (2002)**

""That's a murderous attack on one individual. I don't want to tell you who it is. It's someone both Ian and I know."" JOHN (1989)

She Bangs The Drums

❝'She Bangs The Drums' is about those brief moments when everything comes together. Like staying up till dawn and watching the sun rise with somebody you love. And then regretting it bitterly.❞ JOHN (1989)

❝I remember writing the chorus of 'She Bangs The Drums' and thinking it was like a Dylan chorus, filtered through The Byrds. I know he's one of the reasons I got to do this job. I'd be flattered at that comparison.❞ JOHN (2002)

Elizabeth My Dear

❝Maybe Simon & Garfunkel vandalised the original, which is 400 years old. I never got to hear that one. We wanted it to be a familiar tune so that people would instantly identify with it and then hear the lyric clearly.❞ IAN (1989)

Fools Gold

❝We didn't play acid house music but we did enjoy that music. We were in London in '88 and we'd go to Shoom and Land of Oz. Not so much John and Reni – they didn't go out then. Me and Mani used to go to clubs.❞ IAN (2002)

❝No way. We were always into dance music. Rock and dance were always side by side as far as I'm concerned. People have this way of categorising. It's ridiculous really. The reason we didn't do a dance thing earlier was that we probably couldn't have handled it. 'Fools Gold' didn't seem like a sudden change for us. It was just like the natural thing to do at the time.❞ IAN (1990)

ALBUMS & SINGLES

"'Fools Gold' is about greed. 'Ave you seen *Treasure Of The Sierra Madre* with Humphrey Bogart? Three geezers who are skint and they put their money together to get equipment to go looking for gold. Then they all betray each other. They all end up dead, don't they? That's what the song is about. It's dead right, man..."

IAN (1989)

"It started with a James Brown thing. I picked it up from Eastern Bloc Records in Manchester. We were there signing copies of 'She Bangs The Drums' when it came out [July 1989].
The manager of the shop said we could take a couple of records each. There was an LP I took with a Black Power fist salute on the cover. I wasn't familiar with the song it came from – 'Funky Drummer' – then. I took it home and wrote a song over it. When we played it, it was the repetition that made it work, that made it what it was. Reni hated it when we chopped it up and got him to play along to it. He felt he was being sidelined." JOHN (2002)

"Everyone thought we were into [German band] Can because of that track. Bobby Gillespie said to me a while back, 'All you lot must have been mad for Can,' and he played me *Ege Bamyasi* [the track 'I'm So Green']. It really does sound like a spastic 'Fools Gold.' But we'd never heard of it then." MANI (2002)

"For me it's been right through the Jackson 5, Motown, Northern Soul, then discovering Parliament and Bootsy Collins. Then discovering Barry White and acid house and dance records. Over the same period we had The Beatles, the Stones, T. Rex, and the Pistols. When I've heard our songs in the studio, when they've just been bass, drums and one guitar line, I'd say they're as danceable as any house record I've ever danced to.
"It's just about creating a groove with space around it. We wouldn't say let's write a funk song. We might end up like the Stones, man, trying to sound black. My favourite records at the moment are reggae and I wouldn't think about making a reggae record. When bands think they can do anything, it's shit." IAN (1989)

ALBUMS & **SINGLES** "

One Love

"We went to see a dolphin in Brighton. It was really sad because it was in a tiny pool. None of us said anything for about half an hour, we just stared at it. It kept going past and turning its head and smiling. It didn't jump at anyone else though, did it? There were loads of people around the pool but it was only jumping up when it saw us.**"** IAN (1989)

"...it's for everyone. It's just thoughts. I have a million thoughts focused on one thing. They're all perpetual motion. If it gets too much, you just block it all out and think of nothing." IAN (1990)

Second Coming

"The next album will be more positive, tidier, looser, better. The idea with the first album was to make each song extremely different from the last but we didn't get it. So that's the aim with the second. We don't want to sound like a band.**"** IAN (1989)

"In a way I'm actually pleased – well relieved – that we got the record out. Because there was a period when I thought it wasn't going to happen." JOHN (1995)

"Well what with all the time wasted by the court case, we didn't actually start making the album until 1992, and it was hard to get the momentum kicked in for a while.**"**

MANI (1995)

"Then we had to find a producer. John Leckie said his heart wasn't big enough for the job so he packed it in. He used to worry a lot. He told us we weren't ready to record but we knew we were. He first heard our music when we were on the dole. He loved us and couldn't do enough for us but he changed. He reckons he's getting on in life and time is money to him now. That's not the way to work." IAN (1995)

"That's the beauty of the album. When we were playing we'd switch off and let something else take over. Some belting ideas came flooding out.**"** **MANI (1995)**

"And after such a whacking delay we thought, 'why rush it?' We were going to be criticised anyway, so we thought we might as well make a good album." JOHN (1995)

"We hardly heard a word out of the record company [Geffen] for two-and-a-half years. They just kept on sending the cheques over.**"** **IAN (1995)**

"Neo-classical, homo-erotic classicism." JOHN (1995)

"... I don't think I tried to make a death-laden record but I do think love, sex and death are the most important things in life.**"**
JOHN (1995)

ALBUMS & **SINGLES**

STONE ROSES *Talking*

❝This is how we wanted it to sound. It's much stronger and we sound like a proper live band. We like it, so there's going to be plenty of other people who do. Whatever response it gets is irrelevant to us. When we first started out I knew we were going to do it. I knew our first album was going to attract attention, inspire people, give them a buzz. I think this will do the same thing, but the scale of what it does is out of our hands. Success is writing dynamic tunes for people and having peace of mind no matter what you do.❞ IAN (1995)

❝It was just over-worked... on the basis of the fact that we weren't a cohesive unit and we were spending just too long in the studio. The luxury of endless hours and endless overdubs meant that the freshness was lost. Some songs on *Second Coming* were the third or even fourth recorded versions; things were lying around on master tapes from the first week of recording and we were choosing... there's no drive there, there's no immediacy.❞ JOHN (1997)

"With the second Roses album, I thought, 'He [John Squire] has to get this out of his system, so I'll let him do that,' because we had another three LPs to do to complete the contract."

IAN ON JOHN'S SONGWRITING DOMINANCE (1995)

"Yeah, he [Reni] bought me an acoustic guitar because he was pissed off that I was pissed off that John wanted to do everything on his own. He just walked in one day, handed me the guitar and goes, 'Fucking 'ave him – one day you'll thank me for it.'**" IAN (1998)**

"There's still a lot more room for improvement but we're heading in the right direction. I've learned that part of the secret is opening yourself up to new types of music, not being so blinkered. I never listened to Hendrix or Zeppelin until much later in life." MANI (1995)

"People who come to the shows, tell you whether it's good or shit. The first album was a lot more immediate, nice three-minute pop songs. But we had to change. Bands have to change. Otherwise they should go and work in a shop.**" MANI (1995)**

"There is a lot of nihilism, yeah." MANI (1995)

"There isn't much sociology on my part. It's all personal. We weren't trying to be relevant. Or poignant. Or topical.**"**

JOHN ON THE LYRICS (1995)

"When the album was finished Geffen said, 'Nice one, let's go to work.' When you're not doing anything, you're not aware of it. It's not someone else's opinion you think of. Geffen said, 'Go away and do it.' That's the way it should be, you can't force it. You can't say, 'Shit, we took too long, we'll do something half-baked.'" MANI (1995)

ALBUMS & **SINGLES**

"It's confidential but there are definitely some raw nerves touched there. It's up to the listeners to make what they will."

JOHN ON THE LYRICS (1995)

"A few of them do go on a bit, but if you've got new tools you're bound to use them. Maybe we did overindulge, but there are a few concise pop songs on there, too." JOHN (1995)

"I think some people were looking for something they were never going to get from this LP. They were looking for something similar to the first LP but we didn't want to become U2 and put the same album out four times. It doesn't really matter what the media think of it. What matters to us is what the people on the street think – and all of them have been well positive." **MANI (1993)**

I've been stopped in the street a few times and told, 'Don't listen to what the press is saying, I love the album.'" JOHN (1993)

"Our partnership wasn't very fruitful between albums. We went away to write together but nothing came of it. I found I was making more progress on my own and Ian said he was quite happy with that. He'd tell me he was sitting at home sending me positive vibes to help with the songwriting. But he could have written some songs himself, yeah." **JOHN (2003)**

"When my daughter Janie came along we had to go away to write, because we couldn't get enough time together on our own. We went to the Lakes, Scotland, but very little came from those trips. We were still great friends. Probably too friendly. Maybe if we'd had a go at each other then it would have been sorted out."

JOHN (2002)

"...we weren't working much as a band, everything was kind of individual. We were jamming together but it wasn't the same... I was getting pissed off waiting, 'cos the drums and bass were down by August or September but I couldn't put any vocals down until after Easter. I had to wait for

John to get all his guitar parts. So it was just me fucking about with the harmonica, Reni on his drums and the engineer on the piano, just playing blues songs all day and night for, like, eight months, waiting for John to come out of his bedroom when he'd written the guitar parts.

❝The thing is, we were tight, we'd rehearsed from June to July 1993 and all the songs were in shape. I thought we could go in the studio and just bang it out in a month. But then we were having to listen to 20 guitar tracks.❞ IAN (1998)

❝**I feel like Reni and Mani never really got a full shot on that LP. I still feel they're the best rhythm section that's come off this rock. I'd love to hear a remix of that LP where you can hear the rhythm section and just one or two tracks of guitars.**❞ IAN (1998)

❝Some things were very live, though. 'Daybreak' was a demo, recorded in this little rehearsal room at a nightclub called Clapton's in Tinthwhistle near Glossop. It started off as an instrumental jam and Ian put lyrics to it back at Rockfield. That's me improvising... that's the sort of thing me, Reni and Mani would play all the time.❞ JOHN (1997)

❝**The high points of *Second Coming* for me are the lyrical content of 'Your Star Will Shine' and the riff to 'Driving South.' I can play it properly now. Quite [Jimmy] Pagey? Yeah. Doesn't detract from the riff, though.**❞ JOHN (1997)

❝...putting the album out at Christmas was just because it was ready. We just thought the idea of timing it to have a Number 1 was cynical music-biz bollocks. And I still stand by the decision to give the first interview with [homeless mag] *The Big Issue*. That was a noble gesture. And just meeting blokes on the street who made a fortune, saying 'Thanks for giving us the best week we've ever had', was worth it for me. As for downplaying our return, we probably forgot how to present ourselves after five years away. We didn't know how to appear cool and accomplished. And we probably didn't care.**" JOHN (1997)**

The Unrecorded Third Album

"I think it'll be much better, we're getting better in the studio for one thing. Everyone is au fait with each other's little quirks and techniques. Personally I was shitting it on the first album. But our songs are getting definitely better and we're gonna keep moving on.**" MANI (1995)**

"We've still a long way to go. That's what I enjoy so much about playing the guitar, there's always something new to learn. The permutations for writing songs must be finite – after all, there's only a certain number of notes to experiment with. But we've got a few years left yet." JOHN (1995)

"[I want to] make the best album of all time.**" IAN (1995)**

Greatest Hits LP (2002)

"Well the painting was already done. It's from back in the day. It dates from 1988/89.**" JOHN (2003)**

"I really didn't have to do that. The engineer I was working with at the time was a big Roses fan so I asked him what he would like to see on a compilation and I compared with a quick list I drew up. We whittled it down and my manager compared notes with Ian's manager and we agreed on a final draft. In listening to the songs the thing that struck me was how accomplished the playing was, particularly on the second album. I had forgotten we had got to that level." JOHN (2003)

ALBUMS & **SINGLES**

Manchester/ Madchester

❝No, there isn't a Manchester scene. We're unlike any other local band. Unless you're a chart band or a hardcore punk band, it's really hard to play at all, but we manage.❞ **ANDY COUZENS (1985)**

❝**Well, a lot of bands in the city dislike us because of the way we are. All we are is a big local band, we're not known nationally. So you get the 'the inflated egos of The Stone Roses' and we have got inflated egos, and that's an important part of being a good group. I don't want to slag anyone, but you don't hear people going, 'God, I fucking hate The Railway Children' because they're not the sort of band you hate, whereas I think we are because we're of some sort of value.**❞ IAN (1988)

❝The Happy Mondays are the best group in Manchester. There's some mental stories going around about them. One story I heard was about the time that they bought a gun from a gun shop sale, took it back to school and sat on the school playing fields all afternoon playing Russian Roulette with it. And when I was a scooter boy, they used to kick my scooter over when I parked it outside the youth club.❞ **IAN (1988)**

❝**Oh, sod that. They're all a generation older than us and those days have gone anyway. If you want to talk about tradition, did you know we're the best band since The Hollies to perform a live broadcast from a certain local radio station?**❞
IAN ASKED WHETHER THE ROSES ARE PART OF THE FALL/SMITHS TRADITION (1987)

❝Its not where you're from, it's where you're at.❞ **IAN (1989)**

"It's this theme of Manchester as grey and moping, this whole poverty-as-romance thing. It's rubbish. The sick thing is that people read that and take up that sort of lifestyle. Sit alone in a bedsit and mope. That scene was set up by Joy Division and New Order." IAN (1989)

"It's only a place. People make too much of it. Regionalism is dangerous – like racism, isn't it?" **RENI (1990)**

"Well it's the truth. It's other people who are intent on making a big deal about where we're from. I believe in people, in real people, wherever they come from and whoever they are."

IAN (1989)

"...it's where we're from, after all. If someone describes us as a 'Manchester band' then factually they're correct." **RENI (1989)**

MANCHESTER/MADCHESTER

"I don't know anything about the other Manchester bands. I couldn't claim to tell you the slightest thing about the Inspiral Carpets." JOHN (1989)

"Well, we wouldn't have seen the same sort of things or been to the same sort of places, but we don't just want to be a Manchester band, we want to be big in London as well. It would be better if we came from Sunderland – 'cos no-one comes from Sunderland, do they?" IAN (1989)

"Yeah, all Manchester's lacking is a beach. If there was a beach, it'd be a great city." IAN (1989)

"When you go and see them, they're exciting live and we're told we are. Probably the be all and end all of it is that some of the Happy Mondays said they like house and dance and we've also said we like it in interviews. Bands are bands, people are people and places are just pieces of dust. Just 'cos you come from the same area doesn't mean you have the same attitude." IAN (1989)

"I'm sure there are a lot of similarities in attitude, but we're not joined at the hip." JOHN ON THE HAPPY MONDAYS (1989)

"We might come from Manchester but we don't see ourselves as a continuation of any Manchester scene. The world doesn't begin and end at the Hacienda and we're interested in reaching the rest of the world." IAN (1989)

"...I thought the 'Madchester' issue of *New Musical Express* was funny. But it's when people assume that we're all one big happy family. The only group we know is the Mondays and what we basically have in common with them is that we listen to the same records, go to the same clubs and wear vaguely similar clothes."

IAN (1989)

MANCHESTER/MADCHESTER

❝If you don't live here and read all the things in the papers, you'd think it was Xmas every day in Manchester. I've met people who have moved here and you see them wandering around the streets wondering where all the mythical sparkle is – and it ain't there. It's just a few clubs on a few nights and a lot of people with a good attitude... and that's it, really.**❞** IAN (1989)

❝I like Liverpool. I know a lot of Mancunians would never say that, but I really like Liverpool.❞ IAN (1989)

❝There's a 50-year-old guy down the Hacienda every Friday gettin' people at it. He's 50 odd, 20 stone... no one laughs at him, he gets on partying! It's not the joy of youth, it's the joy of being alive. Live fast. Die old!**❞** IAN (1989)

❝Well look, we've never gone out of our way to align ourselves to the so-called Manchester scene. We've never understood the supposed connection between us and all these other bands. It's a media thing. Everyone's talking about rock and dance music coming together all of a sudden. Well that's bollocks! Everyone I know has always listened to both kinds of music. It's not a sudden thing that's happened...❞ IAN (1990)

❝With us and the Mondays, we were really into house music, and I loved all that. All these bands aren't into any of that or any of the community thing. They seem to me to be the kids who weren't into dancing, so I don't think they've really progressed anywhere.**❞**

IAN (1995)

❝I would end up with [Shaun] Ryder and the crew back at my house after the Hacienda. John was never a club fiend. Me and Ian both loved house music so much. John was more a guitar man. We'd be up all night. I'd be fucked. Then Squire would be giving me the frown the next day at rehearsal and I'd be like, 'I've been out researching music! I'm not just getting off me tits and dancing, I'm thinking of things to pinch, man!' That's where things like 'Fools Gold' originated. The bass line

is inspired by Young MC's 'Know How' which was a tune we were really vibing off at the time. "

MANI (2002)

"No, I don't remember doing drugs with the Happy Mondays and we didn't really hang about with them at all. People think the two bands were joined at the hip for some reason, but I only met Bez at the Hacienda and then we met the rest of the group on *Top Of The Pops* one time and that was about it really. And I haven't seen the film either, but they sent me a release form so I could authorise scenes but I didn't bother. Which is probably why we didn't appear in it at all. " **JOHN ON THE *24 HOUR PARTY PEOPLE* FILM (2002)**

"Football hooliganism got finished overnight, just the strength that we felt with each other, that you can all learn from each other, just en masse, you know what I mean, beautiful. We've always been into dancing in Manchester. It didn't take ecstasy to teach us how to dance, but them days, the community thing, y'know? We've had the Tory government, we've had the miners' strike, here's the people all laughing and dancing. You're trying to finish us but look at us. " IAN ON THE LATE EIGHTIES (2000)

"Things changed when the guns came in. As the drugs get dirtier, in come the guns. From 1989-90 things changed really fast. I was up at Moss Side Carnival and I watched the Cheetham Hill gang walk through in formation, eight strong in rows, each man with a holster. This is June 1990, this is a different day. It's like America, the way the ghettos of America were flooded with crack and coke, and so were the ghettos of England, and the gangs and the guns are going to come up. Where there's drugs there's money – and where there's money, anything goes. " **IAN (2000)**

Stoned &
On Stage

❝That's because the only way to break outside Manchester is a record and I don't think 'Sally Cinnamon' is representative of what we're like live. Playing live is how we'll win people over.❞ **IAN (1988)**

❝...I've read little fanzines from around here and they've said The Stone Roses are hammy, over-the-top entertainment. Well, we're not like one of those little indie groups that are dead precious about their own songs, because I think we have got good songs, but we also know how to deliver the songs. It's a waste of time having good songs if you don't know how to deliver them.❞ IAN (1988)

❝People will be sorry if they don't come and see us. We're so good. I wish I was in the audience sometimes.❞ **IAN (1985)**

❝They were packed out. At the first one there was about a thousand people – it was where we got our crowd from.❞

IAN ON THE 1985 WAREHOUSE GIGS (1989)

❝It was for people who liked staying out all night after the Hacienda. I mean we wouldn't go onstage till about four or five in the morning. It was all Manchester people.❞ **JOHN (1989)**

❝There was one night for example when we were playing under Piccadilly Railway Station and the police were outside threatening to break up the party. To be honest, the situation got a little crazy because they miscalculated as to how everyone would react. **We went on stage just as the tension was about to explode and managed to defuse the bomb with our set but it was touch and go for a while. Unfortunately, that marked the end of the warehouse scene in Manchester.**   IAN (1987)

"I'd jump off the stage in the early days. I was always walking round the crowd singing. When we started getting known we didn't enjoy the shows as much because I had to stay on the stage but in the early days I sang to the girls to get the lads wound up. I'd put my arm round their girlfriends. 1985, '86, '87, everywhere we went, I used to get on that. And it worked – people remembered us.**"**

IAN (2002)

"The best one was a gig in Sweden on that little tour that had been set up for us by Ki the Eye – someone Ian had met while he was hitch-hiking around Europe. We lived in his flat in Stockholm for a couple of months and did five gigs. One night we were doing our set, which was about 40 minutes long. We'd done about 20 minutes and there was nobody there as usual. Then all these women in cleaning

STONED & ON STAGE

overalls came in and just lined up watching us at the back for five minutes. Then they started folding up the tables and chairs and sweeping the floor while we were powering towards the end of the set.** JOHN (2002)

Yeah, a mad night, but all the gigs were. The night in Sweden where Ian sucked the barrel of a gun some nutter pulled, or the night the police showed and arrested the whole audience just before we went on...

ANDY COUZENS ON THE MCGONAGALS GIG, DUBLIN, 1986 (2001)

If you play the same set over and over again in the same atmosphere, you could get fed up with it. It's not very interesting, is it? The purpose of our live performances is not to reproduce the record. IAN (1989)

I don't agree with an attitude like expecting an encore unconditionally. That would be proof that rock music has become showbusiness. JOHN (1989)

I agree with John. As we were saying, loads of bands play the encore at the gig in spite of their awful attitude, this is common sense really. People seem to expect the encore automatically, but that's a big mistake, I think. When the communication between the band and the audience is fulfilled, we are willing to come back on stage and give them a blow again. IAN (1989)

Our former manager claims it was all a set-up to launch us, similar to The Sex Pistols and The Rolling Stones... but the show had never had a live band on before and the sound just broke down, simple as that. But what's really interesting is, two minutes before we went on, I looked at the others and I knew they didn't want to do it... we said a little prayer that something would come and get us out of it and it did. The sound cut out and we were free.

IAN ON THEIR HEADLINE-GRABBING SHORTENED
LIVE SET ON BBC2'S *LATE REVIEW* (2000)

"We were told we had some support slots in Canada with The Rolling Stones if we wanted them. But fucking hell, we're not opening for them. They should open for us. It's obscene that they're even touring. It's a shame they haven't got any friends willing to tell them to quit... there was a time for three or four years when the Stones were red hot. They looked good, sounded good and meant what they were playing. Now they're nothing but a money machine. Sad, really."

IAN (1989)

"We wanted to play Blackpool to give people a day out to finish their summer. When you've got no money and you live in Manchester, there's nowhere to go, it's the local seaside resort. I've been beaten up a few times in Blackpool. At night if you don't wear a tie you won't get into a pub, and if you're walking the streets people bang into you... I'm dying to get on. There's a great atmosphere: 4,000 people have come here for the day; hung out on the fair and on the beach. They're gonna' see The Stone Roses and then go and have a party." IAN (AUGUST 1989)

"It wasn't crap. It was under par. We were struggling all night against the sound as everyone knows. There were a lot of nothing moments but there were a lot of good moments, too!"

IAN ON THE ALEXANDRA PALACE GIG, 25TH NOVEMBER (1989)

"It was crap. It was a disaster." **MANI COMMENTING ON THE SAME GIG (1989)**

"We played an hour and a half last night and they still commented that it wasn't long enough. These are the longest sets we've played." JOHN (1990)

"You'll never see us do a full-scale tour. You can't give your best, can you? Four days in and you'll be like that (slumps forward). A cabbage going through the motions."

IAN BROWN, SPIKE ISLAND PRESS CONFERENCE (1990)

"We asked our manager Gareth to find us somewhere near loads of people and he found us Spike Island. We're not making any money out of it. It's costing us £400,000 to put on and we're getting tish." IAN (SPIKE ISLAND PRESS CONFERENCE 1990)

"For everybody who was there, we weren't actually playing to them, we were just partying with them. And there were a lot of people there partying, 28,004 if you want. It was just up to us to provide a soundtrack to it, if you like. We were just a very small part of a very big event because it's the people who make it an event, it's not just the group. I don't see us as performing. I see them as performing to us and us performing to them, if you know what I mean? And we get off on what they do and they get off on what we do! It's a mutual experience." **IAN ON SPIKE ISLAND (1990)**

"I hated Spike Island. We had lots of rows with management before we went on and we were really angry at the way the show had been managed. It was supposed to be our gig, but the bouncers were taking food and drink off the fans as they walked

STONED & ON STAGE

inside, which we didn't want. They were also pushing the ticket prices up and we kept pulling it down and then we found out they'd employed kids and paid them very little to clean up dirty condoms and needles after the show. It was *horrible...*" JOHN (2002)

"Really good. We sounded dead strong. Was it weird? Nah, it was just like the rehearsal room but with loads of people."

IAN BROWN ON THE FIRST ROSES GIG IN FIVE YEARS (OSLO, APRIL 1995)

"We'll probably bring 'Fools Gold' in. We'll add more songs all the time. But you heard it tonight. None of them deserve dropping. Come and see us in Paris or Glastonbury. We'll be rockin' by then all right." JOHN, SAME GIG (1995)

"Yeah, it's been a bit tight only having Robbie [Maddix] for two weeks, but it's going really well. We've sorted out the set, but we haven't timed it yet. Ian reckons it's an hour and a half. We aren't gonna do that Mary Chain 20-minute thing. It'd be taking the piss. Besides, I really like playing. It used to really annoy me when we'd just get into 'Resurrection' and then have to go off."

JOHN, SAME GIG (1995)

"It's the most enjoyable gig we've ever done."

MANI ON THE BAND'S APPEARANCE AT THE FEILE FESTIVAL, CORK, IRELAND (AUGUST 1995)

"We'd like to be able to charge people 50p or nothing to get in. Concerts are getting really over-priced these days." **MANI (1995)**

"We want to do shows in a marquee like we did for our last Glasgow gig, where it's so hot the sweat goes up to the roof and then comes down like rain. Proper times, they were." IAN (1995)

"It's very nostalgic coming back here, because this is where it started in a way. I think a lot of the people who were involved realised when they got here last time (1989) that it was a serious thing. You get here and you know you're in Japan – you're not in Sheffield or Leeds, loading the van. We never got to America the first time around so this was like the summit.**"** JOHN IN JAPAN (1995)

"Yeah we played to 12 people in Cardiff and six months later it was 6,000 at the Empress Ballroom. We fully expect that to happen in America. It's just a matter of having confidence and self-belief."

MANI (1995)

"It's not going to be hard work. Working down a pit is hard work. It'll be great, playing tunes and the lift you get from that.**"**

IAN ON CRACKING AMERICA (1995)

"No they don't deserve us. We'll go anywhere really, but America really doesn't deserve us, they're fuckin' wankers."

MANI (1995)

"Playing tonight in front of 9,000 people will be a buzz. But going home and seeing me boy will be a bigger one.**"** IAN (JAPAN 1995)

STONED & **ON STAGE** **"**

STONE ROSES *Talking*

"We're going to do more gigs in a year than we've done in eight. The laziest band in pop finally get stuck into some fucking spadework." MANI (1995)

"They'll all be after my blood. I appreciate a lot of people bought tickets for Glastonbury just to see us, but there's not a lot we can do about it, is there? I'm as gutted as they are. I've never been to Glastonbury and I always wanted to wait until we'd done it as a band. This was gonna be the big introduction...**"**

IAN ON THE ROSES' CANCELLATION OF THEIR APPEARANCE AT GLASTONBURY 1995 BECAUSE OF JOHN SQUIRE'S BROKEN COLLARBONE

"If John was fit and the others were up for it, I'd do it. If the organisers asked us to do it, we'd do it, yeah. We wanted to come back with a big bang and that's what was gonna be so good about Glastonbury, but Reading might be the way to do it. Start all over again.**"** IAN (1995)

"Our shows are great because we're so great. It feels right, we've always wanted to do more." MANI ON THE UK TOUR (NOVEMBER 1995)

Politics & Revolution

"Yeah, everybody should be a millionaire. Everybody on the planet." IAN (1989)

"I don't usually think about anything while I'm onstage, but about halfway through the set, I suddenly realised I'd been in this place before. All through the soundcheck, I hadn't recognised it but I blagged my way in here years ago to see Tony Benn at the Labour Party conference… I always thought the aristocracy should be shot. I was brought up that way. And I had a lot of respect for Tony Benn because he was born into the aristocracy but he'd been strong enough to leave it all behind. His speech was really good, he'd completely jumped the gun with his thoughts. Tony Benn deserves more fucking respect than any pop group. It would be a miserable day if I believed any different." IAN (AUGUST 1989)

"Our aims are to reconcile the Russians and the Americans and eradicate diseases and… that's about it. I can't think of anything else." JOHN (1989)

"We're quite happy to speak about politics. We don't give a fuck but we do if you see what I mean. We have a social conscience. The business of just dousing yourself in a trance – forget it."
IAN (1989)

"Thatcher should have gone up in the Brighton bomb."
IAN (1989 PRESS CONFERENCE)

POLITICS & REVOLUTION

"Maggie [Thatcher] and the Royal Family. Six hundred years of piss-taking is long enough, don't you agree?" MANI (1989)

"[The Queen Mother] seems to be aware of the hypocrisy of what she's doing. I think that's so patronising." IAN (1989)

"We're all anti-royalist, anti-patriarch. 'Cos it's 1989. Time to get real. 'When the ravens leave The Tower, England shall fall,' they say. We want to be there, shooting the ravens." IAN (1989)

"Just a bunch of cattle rustlers, the Royal Family." JOHN (1989)

"… I'd like to see him dead. I'd like to shoot him. He owns acres and acres of land, with big houses he's never seen. And there are people living in squalor in some of those places. I have no sympathy at all." IAN ON PRINCE CHARLES (1989)

"The Royal Family is unnecessary to attract tourists. In this country there has been history and the tradition which arouses people's interest as a basis. It's unfair that one individual owns so much private property and is living gracefully, don't you think? I should shut my mouth now otherwise my name might be on the National Front blacklist." IAN (1989)

"We've already had *The Sun* on our backs. They were outside me mam's house all week tapping on the window because of what we said about the Royal Family nine months ago in an interview. I said there wouldn't be a revolution in England unless someone put a bag over the Queen Mother's head. And I said I'd do it. I think Buckingham Palace should be turned into flats for old people who live in cardboard boxes, because that's common sense. So *The Sun* knocked on our neighbour's door and said, 'Do you know that Ian that lives next door? Well he wants to kill the Queen…'" IAN (1989)

"The American Empire – smooth and subtle." IAN (1989)

"…you can't dismiss the whole continent and everything it's done but it can't be healthy for it to stamp its identity on every other country in the world, which it seems to try and do." JOHN ON AMERICA (1989)

"The other day I had these Jehovah's Witnesses come round to my house, and they tried to convince me that the Pope was the Devil's representative on earth. So I told them that Jesus was the world's first communist. So they left. They were genuinely enraged.**"**

IAN (1989)

"The sooner the differences between cultures and traditions are eroded, the better for everybody."

IAN (1989)

"Hell is being stuck in a lift with Elton John and the Queen Mother.**"**

IAN (1998)

POLITICS & **REVOLUTION**

"(The) British Empire. A bunch of public schoolboys playing about. They still give 'em (MBEs) out and there's no British Empire any more. And the Empire was stolen and people were murdered. The British were the first people to set up concentration camps, in the Boer War and in India. They don't tell you these things. They stick up statues in Pall Mall, but they don't tell you the guy just sat in a bunker and sent other people off to shoot and get shot. But there are still statues of them and it's rammed down every schoolboy's throat, our glorious past.

"If ordinary people want these people as their heroes, then let them keep them. Winston Churchill. He's the guy that sent the army to shoot miners in 1924, 'cos they went on strike. He's seen as one of the greatest men in British history and I think that sucks." IAN (1989)

"We don't see pop music as a way of changing things anyway. That's not what we set out with the group to do at all. If we really wanted to change the world, we'd be involved in politics." **JOHN (1989)**

"I still think there could be a revolution in England, it'll just take time, because it's only 45 years that the working class have been able to get an education. And that's where it starts." IAN (1989)

"Would we ever write a song about the environment? I don't know. I saw Sting on German TV and he looked really patronising, like a teacher. I think that could put people off issues like that, but I'll say what I think about anything. What do I think about the environment then? You should stop killing whales and dolphins, for a start." **IAN (1989)**

"Great. It was like five lads keeping the whole of England at bay. It took a lot of strength. Anyone who has a go is a folk hero in Manchester."

IAN ON THE STRANGEWAYS PRISON RIOT (SPIKE ISLAND PRESS CONFERENCE 1990)

"We don't want a ritual slaughter as a support act."

PRESS STATEMENT AS THE ROSES PULL OUT OF A POP FESTIVAL IN NIMES
WHICH IS PART OF THE LOCAL BULLFIGHTING SEASON (1990)

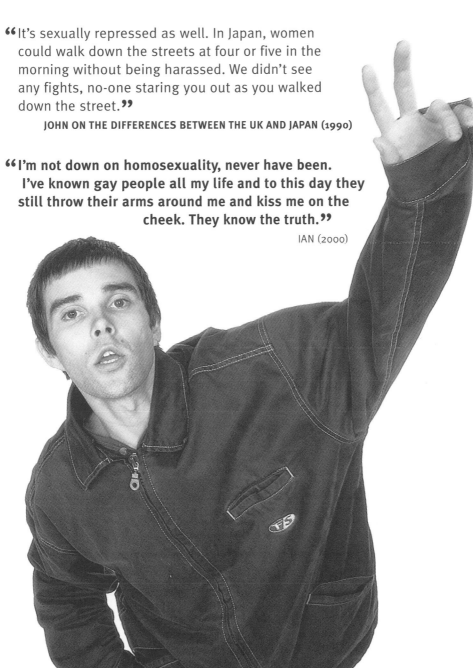

❝It reaffirmed beliefs I had about our own culture. Britain's just a little toy town with a lot of people riding on the backs of most people. And this stupid Royal Family. I can't understand it.❞

IAN ON VISITING JAPAN (1990)

❝It's sexually repressed as well. In Japan, women could walk down the streets at four or five in the morning without being harassed. We didn't see any fights, no-one staring you out as you walked down the street.**❞**

JOHN ON THE DIFFERENCES BETWEEN THE UK AND JAPAN (1990)

❝I'm not down on homosexuality, never have been. I've known gay people all my life and to this day they still throw their arms around me and kiss me on the cheek. They know the truth.❞

IAN (2000)

Art For Art's Sake

John Squire's Paintings

"I did painting at school. I've always made things – Plasticine and Airfix kits. Writing songs is just a natural progression from that." JOHN (1989)

"I copied [Jackson Pollock] because I assumed it would be impossible to get permission to use one of his originals on a record cover. I just copied him and quite enjoyed doing it. And then Reni wanted it doing to his kit. Then we did the guitars as well." JOHN (2002)

"My incentive at the moment is the sleeve for the next single and the four songs for it. I usually tend to take one element of the lyric and magnify it for the painting. This time it's dolphins because Ian sings, 'I'm no dog. I'm a dolphin/I just don't live in the sea.'" JOHN (1989)

"We wanted Jackson Pollock's paintings on the covers but they cost three quarters of a million each." IAN (1990)

"I've been painting for quite a while. It's a messy business. Normally the paintings are quite small but I prefer to work bigger. The biggest canvas I ever painted was in the front room and there was just enough room around the canvas to walk around it. I never sell my paintings. I roll them up and keep them because I love them." JOHN (1989)

ART FOR ART'S SAKE

" The story behind the lemons on the cover [of the first album] is that when we were in Paris, we met this 65-year-old man who told us that if you suck a lemon, it cancels out the effect of CS gas. He still thought that the government in France could be overthrown one day, he'd been there in '68 and everything. So he always carried a lemon with him so that he could help out at the front – what a brilliant attitude. **"** IAN (1989)

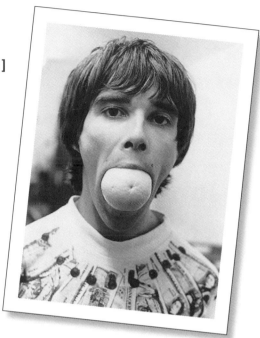

" It seemed like they're destroying a lot of places in town. There's an old cinema in Oxford Road that was a really wicked looking building. It'd been boarded up for a bit but I always thought it might be a club or something. But McDonalds fucked it. They're building a drive-in here in Chorlton as well. It's been going on for ages, though, since the 1930s and Hollywood. **"**

**JOHN ON USING THE STARS AND STRIPES AND THE UNION JACK
AS PART OF A LIVE BACKDROP FOR 'WATERFALL' (1989)**

" I've never tried to pass my paintings off as my own. I'm trying to do me own stuff now, though. I've stopped dripping and splashing. **"** JOHN (1990)

" I wanna make... a prawn. Out of scrap metal... a big prawn out of scrap steel and then spray it with salt and leave it outside and let it go rusty. I thought 'scrap steel seafood' was a good, er, sentence. And when I used to live in Chorlton there was a short cut through

Beach Road and someone there had these... monsters that he'd made, out of girders and exhausts and railway tracks and stuff. **"** **JOHN (1995)**

Drugs & Drink

"If you think of four Brooke Bond chimps on very strong drugs, then that would be very close to how we were." MANI (2002)

"Not wishing to upset anyone's mum and dad, I remember being present for John's first acid trip. This was about '83, at his old flat on Zetland Road. Me and Cressa (Steve Cresser) had these trips and we all did them listening to 'Loose' by The Stooges. It made us feel really freaky. Then we walked into town tripping our tits off. We bought these big Chocolate Feast ice-lollies and we were walking around in a right state with chocolate all over our faces, seeing rabbits and all kinds of shit. We were very naughty boys. We used to wind people up. We were deadly unserious but making this very serious music." MANI (2002)

"I was about two! My mum and dad were out and I just went crawling around, got into the cabinet and sloshed some spirits down. They came back to find me sliding off the couch." MANI (1995)

"None of us drank alcohol." ANDY COUZENS (2001)

"We'd be round at each other's houses – smoking the bong all the time. There was a lot of that going on. We all used to love a trip. Reni had the occasional one but it would send him a bit bonkers. He didn't need drugs – he was already surreal." MANI (2002)

"We went last year and the party was on the *Brookside* set. We got into Harry Cross's house and rolled up some of those funny cigarettes on his settee. He thought it was hilarious."
IAN ON THE ROSES AT THE BROOKSIDE PARTY (1988)

DRUGS & **DRINK**

"...we played the Ad-Lib Club last month. The first time we played it was an anti-heroin benefit... we went on speeding out of our minds. No, we are anti-drugs – except for speed and cannabis, that is."

IAN (1985)

"I don't take so many amphetamines anymore. I used to try and provoke a reaction from the audience. I'm not so up my own arse now, I'm more into the music." IAN (1988)

"The E-scene is just going to explode this summer, people in the media just don't realise how massive it's getting in the provinces." **MANI (1989)**

"None. I don't think drugs change you. Smoking weed can make you more aware of yourself, that's all. It's like anything. Use it, don't abuse it." IAN (1995)

"Yeah, paracetamol is really useful." **JOHN (1989)**

"...we don't go to pubs. We don't even drink beer..." IAN (1989)

"You should experience everything at least once. I read a letter in the *Daily Mirror* today which said, if only scientists would invent something that was a sex aid for men in pill form, then men would be so relieved. Send this guy some ecstasy, man, then he'd be all right." IAN (1989)

"I can't remember... not that many, I never took four at a time. That was like 'how many pints can you drink?'"

IAN ON HIS ECSTASY CONSUMPTION (1995)

"We ended up at The Milk Bar in London one night and everyone was jumping about and, to me, the tune they were jumping about to was just a hairdryer switched on and off. And I was walking about seeing everyone gurning. 'It's coming on, it's coming on now' and all that, and it was sad. And then I was down at the Hacienda

 **STONE ROSES** *Talking*

about two days later and we just started going 'E is shit.' 'Yes it's shit, isn't it?' It was like a Roman thing, y'know? One minute it was like 'E!,' the next it was, 'Not E!' 99

IAN ON GIVING UP ECSTASY (1995)

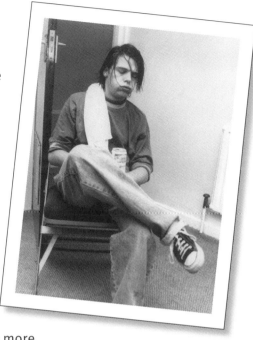

66 **Why do people get into smack? Because they've got fuck all to do. They've got 24 hours to kill.** 99 MANI (1995)

66 I made the mistake of using cocaine for a while, thinking it would make me productive, but it just made me more unsure, more paranoid. 99 **JOHN (1995)**

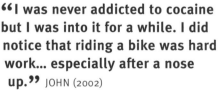

66 **I was never addicted to cocaine but I was into it for a while. I did notice that riding a bike was hard work... especially after a nose up.** 99 JOHN (2002)

66 Each to their own but at the end of the day drugs are destructive, they'll destroy you. They'll take all-comers. The biggest minds fall into rocks, they don't care who they are. Drugs definitely played a part in the destruction of the Roses. I'd apportion the blame on each one of the four of us, we are all to blame. 99

IAN (2000)

"The name was a contradiction – something hard and something pretty, something noisy but tuneful."

"Maybe we'll end up as four Leslie Crowthers with shiny suits and Grecian 2000."

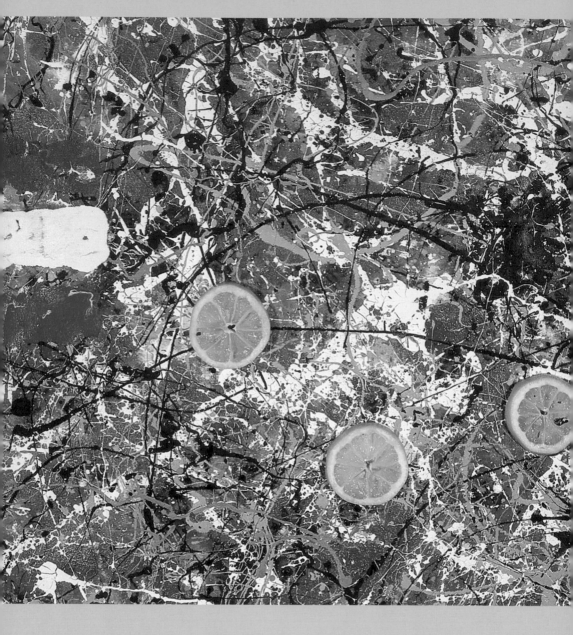

"We wanted Jackson Pollock's paintings on the covers but they cost three quarters of a million each."

"Yeah, we George Best-ed it, for sure. We had it all and we threw it all."

Fame, Fortune & Philosophy

"The respect and musical integrity of the Bunnymen with the Wham! bank account would be ideal.**"** **RENI (1985)**

"If I thought we were going to remain selling 2,000 records, I'd give in now. But I seriously think we're gonna be huge. You can't keep a good band down." IAN (1988)

"It didn't happen overnight. It took five years. Five years of rehearsals and shitty cassettes, and slightly better demo tapes. We were looking at The Pistols and The Beatles and The Byrds and thinking we could have a go at them. We would just try and compete on that level. I couldn't really see any point in aiming low.**"** **JOHN (2002)**

"I don't see us being in that rock 'n' roll tradition at all. In fact I don't like rock 'n' roll. The attitude and leather jacket. It's old hat. It's redneck. Think about it, all the biggest rock groups in the world are rednecks, white Anglo-Saxons: Bon Jovi, Guns N' Roses, U2. The frightening thing is people all over the world relate to that rubbish. Guns N' Roses especially. One of the songs on their LP goes on about 'stupid faggots,' and that album was Number 1 in America. How far back have we gone when a pop group can put rubbish like that in people's heads?" IAN (1989)

FAME, FORTUNE & PHILOSOPHY

"When 'Made Of Stone' was Single Of The Week (*NME*), that was when we realised that the press knew we existed. We'd already sold out Inter 1 and 2 and the Hacienda. At that time we could play anywhere in Manchester, but in London we'd maybe get 200 people. After 'Made Of Stone' it went POW! And you couldn't get into London gigs. It felt right, it felt natural, it felt like we were in the right place at the right time.**"** IAN **(1990)**

"We're not worried about anything. Having a Top 40 hit isn't anything to be worried about, is it? Worry is about having no money, worry is about being hungry, worry is about having nowhere to live, worrying about not being able to get a job when you want one. Worry isn't doing your own thing and getting paid to do it, is it?" IAN (1989)

"Some people say that we're a lad's band. Some say we're a 16-year-old-girls' band. They say a lot, don't they? But they say fuck all...**"** IAN **(1989)**

"The biggest change I've noticed is on a business level. In the past record companies have been very suspicious of us wanting to encroach on what they see as their territory, to design our own sleeves and that kind of thing. Of course, things still happen beyond out control. Like the old company releasing 'Sally Cinnamon', which we resent." JOHN (1989)

"The most extreme thing that happened had to be that guy who was telling me how he was knocked down by a car in London in the spring and had gone into a coma. He said they'd played the album to him and he'd come round. He was thanking me for saving his life and all that. There were tears in his eyes when he walked away.**"**

IAN **(1989)**

"People analyse and look too deeply into what we do. If something's there, I'm not always going to say, 'Right y'are, there is something in there.' I want people to draw their own

FAME, FORTUNE & **PHILOSOPHY**

interpretation. I don't like people who ham it up and rabbit on about themselves. I don't particularly enjoy talking about myself. I'd rather talk about what someone else is up to, where they're at, what they see.**"** IAN (1990)

" Have you found us arrogant and difficult? I don't think we are. What it boils down to is that if someone asks us a dumb question we just don't bother answering it. Too many groups feel they have to play up to people all the time.**"** **IAN (1989)**

"We fully admit we've got this reputation for being awkward. That's the price you pay when you're just strong-willed enough to not always do what people ask you." MANI (1989)

" I'm not particularly keen, but I'm aware that it could, probably will, happen. I'm aware that there's people who'll use my face to fill their wallets, who can suck me in then, when they wanna, shit me out again.**"** **IAN ON BECOMING A SEX SYMBOL (1989)**

"I'm 24 now, too old to be doing what I'm doing. Why am I doing it? Can't think of anything else to do – I'm stuck with it now, huh! The others all consider themselves too old, yeah, they're 23, 24. Yeah, we've missed the boat." IAN (1989)

" We don't mind how people perceive us. In many ways we have just happened. People seem to feel we should be suspicious of this new-found popularity, but why? We like our music so why shouldn't everyone else? If you've been a Stone Roses fan for five years it doesn't make you any better than someone who picked up on us two weeks ago. A couple of years ago there was no LP around and we'd hardly done a gig outside Manchester.**"** **IAN (1989)**

"Nothing's contrived. As far as we're concerned, we've always been like that. We got as far as we have by being stubborn, unfashionable, honest to ourselves. It's not that we tried to re-invent ourselves. Inevitably we've changed in certain ways. People always refer to our past as dodgy. Well most bands have dodgy pasts. At least we grew up in public and made our mistakes in public." JOHN (1990)

"Hunky? I don't know about that. I'm too thin. All right then, I am. The rest of the group are all really hunky. We're accidentally hunky." **IAN (1989)**

"**I was on the tube the other day when it was rush hour and I noticed some bloke staring at me. So I stuck me tongue out at him. That's what people have got to expect if they stare at us, and we've got to expect people staring at us after we've been on telly. I mean, we're working dead hard at the moment to destroy our privacy, I suppose. Funny that.**" IAN (1989)

"...we're the most important band in the world because we've got the best songs and we haven't even begun to show our potential." **IAN (1989)**

"**I wish there'd been a group like The Stone Roses around when I was 16... I think we're relevant, we're important. I think we're exciting, mind-expanding! Just that! I know I'm blowing me own trumpet!**" IAN (1990)

FAME, FORTUNE & PHILOSOPHY

"We're gonna be bigger than The Beatles, The Rolling Stones and Madonna put together." STONE ROSES (1990)

"We're men on a mission." IAN (1990)

"I want as many people as possible to hear it. I want us to be huge everywhere." **IAN (1990)**

"You've got to make sure you don't turn into a twat." IAN (1990)

"People tend to settle for a fiver instead of going for the pot of gold." **IAN (1989)**

"I believe in living for the moment." IAN (1990)

"I spent a day crawling round me house on me belly so no-one could see me. It was a terraced street, but there was a garage opposite with a skip outside it and there were four girls sleeping behind the skip. They'd get up in the morning and try knocking on the door and the windows and peering through the letter box. They were shouting the name of the cats through the door because they'd read them in *Smash Hits*. I had to crawl to the phone to ask my girlfriend to bring milk home from work 'cos I couldn't get out to buy it." JOHN RECALLS THE PRESSURES OF FAME (1995)

"We should be on *Top Of The Pops*. I like seeing our record go up and Kylie and Phil Collins go down. There's no point moaning about them.

You've got to get in there and stamp them out. Because I believe we have more worth.**"** IAN (1989)

"We don't care if our records go to Number 9, it doesn't mean nothing. If they go to Number 1, it does. It needs more than just one group to change things, it needs loads of them. If we give strength to people then it's good.**" IAN (1990)**

"We're against hypocrisy, lies, bigotry, show business, insincerity, phonies and fakers... there's millions of them and they're all pricks. People like Jagger and Bowie... they're so insincere now they're just patronising." IAN (1990)

"If I was sat in a cafe and someone came up to me and said, 'Eh mate, what do you think you'll be doing in five years time?' I'd go 'Eh, what'll *you* be doing when you're 60?' It's not a legitimate question, it's a stupid question.**"**
IAN BROWN, SPIKE ISLAND PRESS CONFERENCE (1990)

"I want to be an astronaut. I want leave the atmosphere and see what the planet looks like from the other side." IAN (1989)

"I'd love to travel at three times the speed of sound. Why? Because I've never done it before.**" JOHN (1989)**

"...the bubble is about to burst, though, isn't it? It's not gonna last, is it? Name me one band that's lasted? The Rolling Stones? Pile of shit, man! That's not lasting is it? That's hanging on. They should be put out of their misery. We don't want to make idiots of ourselves like that. Basically, if we come out of this with no self-respect, then we've failed, man. It wouldn't mean anything. Nothing." IAN (1990)

"Somebody was going to make money off us coming back, so it was the best thing to do. The last time the *NME* had us on the cover it was one of the biggest-selling issues of the year. We'd rather the money went to the homeless than into the coffers of a big organisation. We thought let's put something back. If somebody

FAME, FORTUNE & **PHILOSOPHY**

gets a house just by the four of us talking then it's got to be worth it. It works better for us as well, because it's away from the music press. **99** IAN ON APPEARING ON THE FRONT COVER OF THE BIG ISSUE (1995)

66 I'd prefer to have money than not, but I won't do this forever if I'm not enjoying it, for the sake of the money. 99 JOHN (1995)

66 I'm not a rich man. I owe a lot of money. Money runs through your fingers and it's gone. Everyone thinks we're loaded, that we're driving around in Bentleys. Let them think it. Every time you see the words Stone Roses, it's Stone Roses £20 million, Stone Roses £40 million, but it's gone. **99** IAN (1995)

66 I've never looked for cocaine and country houses and hanging out with bands and celebrities. I've never been interested or wanted it or done it. 99 IAN (1995)

66 The aim is to do as much for people as you can and not become a martyr to the cause. We'll never lose touch. And we'll never sell out and play Wembley, either. **99** IAN (1995)

66 Well I don't need any more. 99 JOHN ON MONEY (2003)

66 Maybe we'll end up as four Leslie Crowthers with shiny suits and Grecian 2000. **99** JOHN (1990)

66 I think early on Liam [Gallagher] said his favourite people were me and his mother. Whatever people think of Oasis, they really did it big and I'm really glad that we influenced them. I know that we never fulfilled our potential, but at least we influenced the biggest group out of England since The Beatles. But first is first and second's nothing and I still think the Roses were better than Oasis, but I'm glad we kicked the door open for them. I'm glad they took full opportunity. 99 IAN (2002)

66 Yeah, we George Best-ed it, for sure. We had it all and we threw it all. **99** IAN (2002)

Flares & Fringes

"They were Goth-ed up in paisley shirts, pointed boots and silly hairdos. 'You've got to look like proper Scallies,' I said. So Johnny sat at home making matching shirts for us, cutting out shapes in potatoes, so for our first gig we all had the same image: mad psychedelic wear with wicked Byrds-style bowl cuts." **MANI (2001)**

"Also, the clothes and haircut were more important than the music for us, so we didn't care about the terrible sound very much."

IAN (1989)

"We're obsessed with clothes, always have been. It's all very important like, for instance – and make sure you get this right – with flares coming back people have got to realise that you can't wear anything wider than 21-inch bottoms. Anything more looks ridiculous." **IAN (1989)**

"I get really snappy if summat don't look right."

MANI ON CLOTHES (1990)

"…we've never meant to be the slave of fashion or the clothes, the music or even the attitude. If you always take notice of what other people do, you wouldn't make anything original. I think some dependent people would follow fashion in order to discover their own identity somehow." **IAN (1989)**

"As for the clothes, we are taking care of them in our own way…"

JOHN (1989)

FLARES & FRINGES

❝I wish people would talk about our French, Spanish and Italian shirts more than our baggy old trousers. The top half of The Stone Roses is continental, the bottom half is Manchester❞ **IAN (1989)**

❝**I think I've got divine knowledge and complete ignorance of everything. Except about clothes. They're [flares] probably just as important as England falling actually.**❞ JOHN (1989)

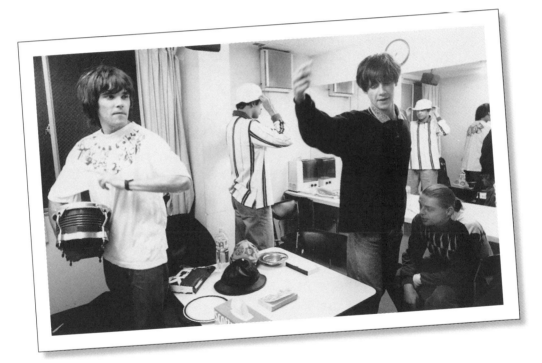

❝Our clothes get more written about than our music. Did we have safety pins in our jackets when we were Sex Pistols fans? No, I don't think so. But I used to have a pair of tight trousers when everyone else had flares on. Painted shirts, I was only about 12 or 13.❞ **IAN (1990)**

❝**It's only Ian who wears flares, actually. The rest of us just wear parallels. Ian's just got this idea that if you walk down the street without being laughed at then you must be doing something wrong. He's a bit mad, though...**❞ JOHN (1989)

"Trousers? Well them three wear parallels but I wear flares, but definitely not over 21 inches. It's ridiculous, you look like a clown. Why do I wear flares? Cause they swing when you walk so it's perpetual motion. It's important for your state of mind. It's also important that they come right down to the bottom of the floor so your shoes are obscured, cause if you've got half-mast trousers on then you look like an idiot as well...

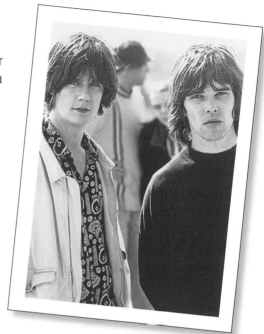

"When you walk down the street with a pair of 21-inch hipsters on, it's like being in the house with your slippers on. I get laughed at more than stared at. It doesn't bother me. I'd rather be laughed at than not, every time." **IAN (1989)**

"I've always been into clothes. When I was 12 I used to wear 21-inch hipsters like these. Then I stopped wearing them for a long time and now I'm wearing them again. Flares are really comfortable. They feel just right. The main reason was because nobody else was wearing them. We'll have to stop wearing them soon because everyone else is. Loads of people who come to see us are wearing flares and parallels. Some of them look better than me in flares. A lot of people don't cut it, though, and they shouldn't wear them just because their favourite group does. They should wear what they look good in." IAN (1989)

"Please tell 'em: FLARES NO MORE. Too many sheep... I got these trousers from Umbros in Glasgow. Only a fiver. And they're 'ipsters, too." **IAN (1990)**

FLARES & FRINGES

"Flares are gone. Never worn flared kecks in me life. Flares are for Oldhamers." MANI (1990)

"The shop I got these in had three pairs the first time, so I bought the lot. I went in last week and they had 200 pairs... I need the jumbo cord to stay ahead... flares are going to be high street by the summer... fashion! Fashion is some bloke rubbing sixpence between his fingers and trying to get your last ten bob out of you.**"**

IAN (1989)

"It's always the same. I grow my hair quite long, and then I get it cut off really short. I just happened to have a crop when the album was released – I didn't grow it out because I thought it was a mistake. I'll do the same – get it cut when it gets longer."

IAN ON GETTING BACK HIS OLD-BAGGY-STYLE HAIRCUT (1995)

"It was a brilliant floppy hat that I used to wear in a lot of photos. It had stripes round it and sun signs on it, very old and faded, but really cool. It was a real trend-setting hat that. But I only ever saw one true sister hat to it. This girl in the Hacienda had it on and we were like, 'Shazam, Kapow!'**"**

**RENI ON HIS FAMOUS HAT GIVEN
TO HIM BY A FAN (1995)**

STONE ROSES *Talking*

Legal Matters

❝We hooked up with him because he's such a character, good to have about.❞ **IAN ON MANAGER GARETH EVANS (1989)**

❝**The first time we met him, he took his bloody underpants off! He was trying to impress us, saying he could sell anything to anyone, anywhere, any time. He was currently selling this range of underpants called Pommes, little white briefs with an apple logo on them. He had a whole box of them in the corner. But he insisted on taking off his trousers and trying to sell us the underpants he was wearing...❞**
JOHN ON GARETH EVANS (1989)

❝It's an important relationship. If people know what you're doing, what you think, what you sound like, then you should give them all of it yourself. You shouldn't have other people doing your sleeves and telling you how your videos should be, dressing you. It should be you. It should be complete.❞
JOHN ON ARTISTIC FREEDOM AND CONTROL (1990)

"We were going to fly to MIDEM originally because we heard they were there. We were going to steam in there, smash the stall up and paint him, but we phoned up and [realised] he'd left a day earlier so we had to wait till Monday. It's not really the record, it's the video. Shot in Manchester, it's got some bloke sitting in Piccadilly Station reading *The Face*... it's fucking insulting.

"He [Paul Birch] had a press release together before the police arrived... we told him we weren't happy with the video. He thinks he's got some sort of immunity because he's in the biz, [he thinks] we're not real people, we're just fucking puppets, performing monkeys that he can earn a buck off. He told us to make an appointment and that's when I kicked off. He's earning a lot of money off us and he tells us to make an appointment. So then we painted him. And his office and his motor. Full tins."

IAN ON THE ROSES ATTACK ON PAUL BIRCH AND THE FM-REVOLVER RECORDS OFFICE (1990)

"It was my idea to do it, but we didn't get very far before we got stopped. They answered the front door of the office and Reni got in first, then the rest of us and we just started chucking paint around, but they locked the door into the rest of the building and called the police. We did a lot of damage and they took us to court and that's when it hit us that we'd done a pretty bad thing. Mani was making jokes about us getting raped in prison.

"We were charged £3,600 each and the judge could have given us a custodial sentence, but he said, in summing up, that the only reason that he didn't give us a custodial sentence was because it could have enhanced our career, so we got off lightly there."

JOHN (2002)

"We're in court in September – you know about that. Don't yer? The money's not been decided yet. They're claiming £23,000, but I don't think it'll come out as that much. It's an over-estimation, definitely." JOHN ON THE FM-REVOLVER CASE (1990)

"I didn't know abstract expressionism was a criminal offence."

JOHN (1990)

LEGAL MATTERS

"It's hardly an outing." IAN ON THE FORTHCOMING FM-REVOLVER TRIAL (1990)

"We shouldn't have been in the dock – we should've been birched!" RENI AT THE END OF THE FM-REVOLVER TRIAL (1990)

"It was the worst hotel I've ever stayed in." IAN ON BEING RELEASED FROM CUSTODY (1990)

"Some bloke from our old record company released an old single we didn't want releasing to make a few more quid out of us and he ended up with paint all over his car... somehow." IAN (1990)

"Well the police woke me up and found a pile of paint-covered clothes next to my bed."

JOHN ON HIS ARREST BY THE WEST MIDLANDS CONSTABULARY AFTER THE ATTACK ON THE FM-REVOLVER OFFICE (1990)

"We didn't know anything about him. We knew he was a plonker, but he said he was going to give us some money."

IAN ON SIGNING WITH PAUL BIRCH AND FM-REVOLVER (1990)

"I'd like to see how The Stone Roses would have progressed with a proper manager." JOHN (2003)

"I'm just glad to stay out of the nick."

JOHN AFTER THE COURT CASE WITH FM-REVOLVER (1990)

"I've been pulled out of cars and handcuffed, thrown in cells then released with no charge, just because I'm Ian Brown." IAN (1998)

"I can understand the indignation you felt, but the way in which you went about it was immature to the point of childishness. I think a prison sentence, suspended or otherwise, might lead to notoriety for you and ultimately be to your benefit and I certainly don't want to contribute to that."

JUDGE MOTT QC'S JUDGEMENT AT THE FM-REVOLVER TRIAL (1990)

"Well, that's the reason that we spent so long between albums – and, yeah, I think that definitely ended our progress. I think that with somebody more trustworthy we'd have had a brighter future."

JOHN (2003)

"Silvertone signed us for 35 years, we'd have only got 10 for armed robbery." **THE STONE ROSES (1990)**

"We've had to fight for everything we can get. It was only when we became successful in their terms that they wanted to sort out a decent contract. We were angry with the company because we considered them to be slow, we considered them to be not sharp enough. They could not understand our potential. It's been a constant battle to get them to appreciate exactly what we are about and where we can

LEGAL MATTERS "

go. It was like a rollercoaster as our name became known and people followed us to gigs. The last 15 to 20 dates were sold out. IAN ON SILVERTONE (1991)

"I'm going to the trial most days and I'm starting to get a bit restless." IAN (1991)

"I remember looking at the very real prospect of never making another record and just doing gigs. We all agreed that if we couldn't get out of the deal we were prepared to take it that far."
JOHN ON THE SILVERTONE LAWSUIT (1993)

"You could get boiling angry about it but animosity makes you weak. Look at Nelson Mandela. He was banged up for 27 years but he just came out and said, 'I bear no grudge to society, no animosity.' How can he do that, you know what I mean? When the Birmingham Six came out, they were fucking angry, rightly angry. But Nelson just came out as Mr Peace."
IAN ON THE SILVERTONE LAWSUIT (1995)

"...undoubtedly one of the worst contracts I've ever seen."
ROSES LAWYER JOHN KENNEDY ON THE SILVERTONE SUIT (1991)

"What it all comes down to is there's no substitute for common sense. After all there is a shared aim to sell as many records as possible." **JOHN KENNEDY (1991)**

"They lost months out of their career and, even with Geffen guaranteeing them some of their costs, it could still have left them very exposed financially. The worst-case scenario was that, if they didn't win, they'd be forced to work with Zomba [Silvertone parent company] again. That's bit like a divorce court telling a couple they have to go back and live together again."
JOHN KENNEDY, ROSES LAWYER (1991)

"We refuse to break our [recording] silence."
STONE ROSES STATEMENT (1991)

LEGAL MATTERS

 **STONE ROSES** *Talking*

"I want at least £1 million. The Stone Roses have a five-album deal with Geffen. If they are successful, it could net them anything up to £50 million. I simply want monies which are owed for the part I played in thrashing out the deal. Right from the start I was out hustling and bustling every day for them."

MANAGER GARETH EVANS (1992)

"Three children were born. We got truckloads of money from Geffen. The court cases – first with the record company, then the manager – lost us momentum. Things came out in the first court case that lost us any faith we still had in the manager, so he went. And the result of the case was us signing with Geffen. So we ended up with no manager, pots of money and three kids. That's the reason we lost momentum." JOHN (1997)

"It saddens me when I go down to the Embankment and see all the homeless people there. We used to go down there quite a bit during the court case. With the Criminal Justice Act taking away squatters' rights, it's going to get even worse."

MANI TALKING ABOUT THE SILVERTONE CASE (1995)

The Honeymoon Is Over

Reni & John Quit

"We hope we'll be together this time next year, and this time in five years, but we can't say. It's a random universe. The band is an entity in itself – I could see us all drifting apart If the band didn't exist." JOHN (1995)

"After lengthy deliberation, it is with great regret that I feel compelled to announce my decision to leave The Stone Roses. I believe all concerned will benefit from a parting of the ways at this point and I see this as an inevitable conclusion to the gradual social and musical separation we have undergone in the last few years. I wish them every success and hope they go on to greater things. My intentions are to continue writing while looking for a new band and to begin working again as soon as possible. Thanks for everything." JOHN'S PRESS STATEMENT APRIL 1996

"I started coming round to the idea that I didn't want to go in for the next studio album and I thought it was fair that I let them know. They didn't accept it initially and thought they could talk me round. I was quite surprised, because I thought it was fairly obvious, the way the tour had gone, that it wasn't fulfilling. On stage was fine but... I thought there's got to be a bit more to this." JOHN (1996)

❝It's just the stuff they were listening to, really. There was initially a kind of common ground in The Beatles and the Stones and all that classic 1960s stuff, then Ian got more and more heavily into rap to the exclusion of everything else and I got more into guitar music in any form that it came, no matter what the trousers and the haircuts were like. I suppose Reni used to have a foot in both camps, but wasn't an elitist in any way with regards to what he would listen to.❞ JOHN (1996)

❝It wasn't an easy decision to make but I do feel it was the right one and I think the future will bear that out.❞ **JOHN (1996)**

❝I didn't believe in the band any more. I realised that the person inside Ian wasn't the person I loved. I couldn't find him. I looked into his eyes and he was a different person. It was a frightening experience. I don't want to stick the knife in. All I can say is that he became a complete stranger. It was bizarre because everyone assumed we were the best of friends, which puts a tremendous pressure on you.❞

JOHN (2002)

❝When I told Ian that I was leaving, it was like, the first time I'd spoken to him in a good few years. I don't really know who he is now. People change, relationships change, hairstyles change, that's life isn't it?❞ JOHN (1999)

❝No one loved or worked harder for that band than me.❞ JOHN (2002)

"We feel as cheated as everyone else who has heard the news. We are in the middle of recording the next LP. We're disgusted, yet feeling stronger and more optimistic than ever.**" IAN BROWN, MANI, ROBBIE MADDIX & NIGEL IPPINSON'S PRESS STATEMENT 29 MARCH 1996**

"Recording *Second Coming* was a nightmare. My father had just died, I was depressed and the band expected me to carry on as normal. Only Reni noticed. Actually, he told me a couple of weeks ago that Squire was after sacking me at that point. Squire thought he was in charge, working everyone with his foot pedal. Ian became guarded. He wanted to push his own songs and Ian felt let down by being excluded from the band and John's life. Reni left because of it, and Robbie Maddix came in two weeks before the world tour. It wasn't the same.**"** MANI (2001)

"Personally, I'm sick of underachieving.**"** RENI (1995)

THE HONEYMOON IS OVER

❝ That's it now I've quit.
I'm not drumming any more.
There's other things going
on but I'm not drumming
now. I've got to prioritise
things at the moment.
I haven't seen my daughter
for four weeks and she's
missing me. I need to go
and see her. **❞** RENI ON
QUITTING THE ROSES (1995)

❝ He [Reni] had very
strong opinions about
everything. He was very
funny as well, but he
was showing all the
signs that he wanted to leave. I'm not
trying to blame him for the delay, but it was apparent he wasn't
really interested. He wasn't there a lot of the time. **❞** **JOHN (1995)**

❝ Time ran its course. The way it is, is the way it is.
He'd had enough so he left. **❞** IAN ON RENI'S DEPARTURE (1995)

❝ Heroin? That's a bit snide. Reni's made a decision and it's bullshit
to even speculate what the reasons might be. It's nobody's
business but his, man. **❞** **MANI (1995)**

❝ I didn't know but I suspected that Reni would leave. He's been ill
and frequently disappeared from the studio. But it was up to him
to say he wanted to quit. I guess he put it off because it was hard
to end. But when he went I knew we could get another drummer
and carry on. **❞** JOHN (1995)

❝ Ian had a row with Reni and came into rehearsal and told me and
Mani that he'd had it with Reni... and that he'd never work with him

again... and that he wanted to see him in the gutter. And we said, 'Hang on a minute, we've got a tour starting in 10 or 12 days.' But I knew from Ian's... I could see in his eyes that if it came to it Ian would walk out. In fact he said, 'It's me or him.' So we had no choice but to look for somebody else. I was determined to tour the album and there's no way I could have done that without the singer.❞ **JOHN (2003)**

❝**Vital. No Reni, no music, no band.**❞ ANDY COUZENS (2001)

❝Prior to that point no member of the band would have been able to make that statement. We did run the band democratically but everything changed from that point on because he held a gun to our head basically. Though strangely I know that Ian told Dave Simpson [of *The Guardian*] that it was me that had the falling-out with Reni and that was the reason he left.❞ **JOHN (2003)**

❝**It [the Roses] became like a stumbling, wounded beast towards the end. It didn't know where it was going or what it wanted.**❞

JOHN (1997)

THE HONEYMOON IS OVER ❞

Robbie Maddix Joins

"I'd heard the album before I joined. I knew about them, so there weren't great expectations. When I met them, walked into the room, I could see they weren't on a star trip. I just said, 'How ya doin?' and we started playing."

DRUMMER MADDIX JOINS THE BAND (1995)

"I wouldn't say it was easy. That's belittling the situation. It wasn't easy, but I've got a good ear and these guys were on their shit and they wanted to do it. One of my first impressions was, 'Well, they might be on a downer over Reni,' but I didn't know the situation. It's a decision that he made and that was it."

ROBBIE (1995)

"It wasn't a piece of cake to join The Stone Roses, but it would have been harder for me to join another group. I produce, I remix, I write songs. My career was already mapped out. I'd moved on from doing sessions like in the early days with Errol Brown and Terence Trent D'Arby. From 1990 I was with Rebel [MC]. After that I became his right-hand man 'cos he wasn't too musical. Same thing here, I want to contribute. I'm here for the duration. I didn't even have to think about it. I wanted to join The Stone Roses." **ROBBIE (1995)**

"I knew 'Fools Gold.' I can't say to you, 'Oh, yeah, I always had the first album.' I don't buy albums." ROBBIE (1995)

"I drove down the rehearsal room. I came out of the car and the three of them were playing 'Daybreak.' I was still outside and it sounded fuckin' enormous. I walked into the room and it was just there, straightaway. You can't put the brakes on it, man, no matter what happened. It's gonna happen, innit?" **MANI (1995)**

THE HONEYMOON IS OVER

Life After Squire

❝We don't jump through hoops for people. We've still got that much integrity.❞ **MANI (1996)**

❝**[Why continue?] Because it's my name, it's Stone Roses music, and that's the important thing. He [John Squire] hasn't wanted to play with the band since 1991. Why does all this have to come out now? Why didn't you ask us? Where do you think we've been all this time?**❞ IAN (READING FESTIVAL PRESS CONFERENCE, AUGUST 1996)

❝John wrote most of the songs on *Second Coming* because we let him do it. John's had his day and now he's gone.❞

IAN (READING, 1996)

❝**I've had rock 'n' roll shit all my life. I'm a guitarist and I write songs and I want to work with people I respect. People were always saying to me 'Yes I'll use you as a – but I'll use you to my advantage.'**❞

AZIZ IBRAHIM ON WHY HE JOINED THE STONE ROSES (READING, 1996)

"Why bother? The sum is more than the parts, although some people don't recognise that. You're all dumb, complete wankers, the lot of you."

MANI ON WHY THE ROSES DIDN'T FOLD
AFTER JOHN SQUIRE QUIT (READING, 1996)

"He wouldn't even bother to phone my house if he heard that my mum, my dad and everyone who ever lived in my village was killed in a plane crash, because he couldn't be arsed to get out of bed."

MANI TALKING ABOUT HIS RELATIONSHIP
WITH JOHN (READING, 1996)

"He became friends with cocaine. Before that he was straight."

IAN ON JOHN (READING, 1996)

"I feel sad that I saw John on stage fucking hanging around with Oasis the other week. Has he joined the Phil Collins/ Paul McCartney club now?" MANI (READING, 1996)

"As for Reading, it was a case of staying loyal to a friend. Ian knew I was going to join Primal Scream but there was no way I'd desert him after John did the dirty." MANI (2001)

"It doesn't affect me personally, but I do think it tarnishes the memory of the band, because we were never about that. You know sniping. It hurts in that way. But I realised when I left that the friendships didn't extend beyond a business relationship anyway, except maybe with Reni. I'm not interested in apportioning blame or getting angry about it. I dunno. Maybe because the thing didn't work without me? But then again, I think it didn't work without Reni, with the benefit of hindsight." JOHN (1997)

LIFE AFTER SQUIRE

The Final Split

❝Having spent the last 10 years in the filthiest business in the universe, it's a pleasure to announce the end of The Stone Roses. God bless all who gave us their love and supported us. Special thanks to the people of Manchester, who sent us on our way. Peace be upon you.❞ IAN (OCTOBER 1996)

❝**After much speculation, I've decided, along with Ian Brown, that it's time to end the Roses saga. I will be joining Primal Scream, who are one of only three other bands I would ever consider joining. I'm absolutely delighted and am relishing the opportunity of playing with Bobby [Gillespie] and my friends. I wish Ian, Robbie, Nigel and Aziz all the best and hope we will work together in the future.**

❝**I take the opportunity to thank our record company who have stood by us through thick and thin and to our fans worldwide for their loyal support. It's been a privilege to give these people a buzz and it wouldn't have been possible without them. I wish Johnny [Squire] and his new outfit a fruitful time. I hope they go on and smash it.❞** MANI (OCTOBER 1996)

❝It ended at Reading, but the cracks first began to show during the 'Fools Gold' sessions. John had doubts about Reni's drumming and thought I wasn't working hard enough. But I couldn't be a robot like John.❞ MANI (2001)

"At the end of the set all I could see were 60-80,000 people with their hands in the air and smiley faces. OK, so the vocals were a bit poor but the *NME* was out to bury us."

IAN TALKING ABOUT READING (1998)

"It was only a couple of days later when I heard the tape. I thought, 'Shit, that was pretty poor.' I'll throw my arms up now and say the vocals on that day were terrible." IAN (1998)

"Unnecessary. Things could have continued. We were sounding good, everyone was up to write another LP, then... I didn't have a choice whether I was carrying on or not." IAN (1998)

"It's a crying shame. We could have achieved so much more. But everything has its natural life and I think it was right that it was allowed to die. We've all gone on and done well, so no regrets. Things happen for a reason and for me the reason the Roses imploded was to go and join the Scream." MANI (2000)

THE FINAL SPLIT

Post Roses

IAN BROWN

Unfinished Monkey Business LP

"Well, the last Roses day was Reading in 1996, and then I spent from January to about September writing songs with Robbie and Nigel with a view to the next Roses LP. But then they were saying, after John left, 'Why don't you go solo? We'll back you up.' So I started thinking about the freedom of going solo and not being restricted by a band. I didn't really want to form another band after the Roses, 'cos it felt like something I'd already done. Then in the winter of 1996 I started thinking, 'I've got to make an LP.' I'm fed up of people coming up and saying, 'Do something, man.' By this time people had heard The Seahorses LP and were saying "It's crap."

IAN (1998)

"In the winter of 1996, I decided I was gonna stay in – not go to any nightclubs, not go to any bars, not waste any time, just stay in until I had 10 or 12 songs done for the record." IAN (1998)

"That bloke from Dodgy was in another studio at the place where we were finishing the last Roses LP. He was asked if he knew anything about it – at the time everyone was making out it was top secret – and he told some journalist that I'd only answer to the name of King Monkey. She printed it and I thought it was funny. Plus they always used to call me Monkey at school, and the press'd sometimes refer to me as 'Simian lead singer.'"

IAN ON THE TITLE OF HIS DEBUT SOLO ALBUM (1998)

"I started making it at home on 8-track. Then me and Aziz transferred it all to bigger studios and built it from there. A lot of it was done on the old desk that some of the Trojan reggae records were made on. There are no effects on the LP – no reverb, no echoes, no fancy stuff. I wanted it all straight. On 'Sunshine' I wanted it to sound like someone sat next to you playing a song without all that digital trickery. Studios can make anyone sound great. I wanted it all to be as real as possible. To be honest, I'm not addressing anyone with this stuff." IAN (1998)

"... I'm up for working with anyone, apart from Elton John. You have to remember that all this is new to me. Working on your own is half the fun and half the grief. I've learned some things about myself. I wasn't really sure I was musical until I started. This has given me the confidence to go on." **IAN (1998)**

"I felt absolutely free. I had no accountants, no managers, no lawyers, no record company. It was just me and my friends making music in a great place. So the studio was a playground in that way. There were no pressures at all, 'cos everyone thought I was finished. They didn't know what I was up to and I loved it. They didn't know where I was, what I was doing." IAN (1998)

POST ROSES

My Star

❝Brought up in the 1970s, astronauts were sold to kids as the
ultimate heroes. Watching a video on the launch of *Apollo 15*,
I was struck with how the whole thing was a military exercise.
Astronauts were former fighter pilots from the US air force; 'Space
exploration, an excursion to the stars, on a military mission, a
military journey to Mars.' Imagine how you'd feel living in the
ghettos and the poor rural areas of America in 1968 – billions of
dollars spent on a rocket to visit a piece of rock in the sky;
'I'll see you in My Star.'❞ **IAN (1998)**

Can't See Me

❝I'm most proud of 'Can't See Me', because that's me on bass
guitar and me doing the lead guitar solo! It's taken from a cassette
Mani was messing around with on a four-track Portastudio.
On the record Reni is credited with drums but Mani assures me
it is actually a breakbeat – Mani plays the melody lead bass so
it's a bass duet! The guitar solo
was played on the same pink
Stratocaster John used on 'I Am
The Resurrection'. **IAN (1998)**

❝**I've got this big pillowcase
of tapes at home of Roses live
shows and rehearsals and stuff,
and I was just going though
them one day and I found this
bassline and remembered it.
So I phoned him [Mani] up and
said, 'Can I put some lyrics
over this for my record?' and
he said, 'Course you can.'**❞

IAN (1998)

Corpses In Their Mouths

❝When I told Aziz I was going solo, he asked if I'd write a tune with him, cause he felt sure we'd work well together. We sat up in my front room one night and had the main bones of the song in about 10 minutes. Aziz took it away and brought it back the next day and presented me with the beautiful playing and arrangement that is 'Corpses'. A truly joint effort where I think we complement each other perfectly. It was written in the same way as most of the early Roses tunes – fresh!❞ IAN (1998)

Ice Cold Cube

❝I had 'Ice Cold Cube', which I'd written on acoustic, so I said, 'We need brand new music behind this.' We'd played it at Reading, but it was too slow, it didn't really go. So we re-organised it, put it in shape and there was another one.❞ IAN (1998)

Golden Greats LP

❝I wanted to make an acid house record, so after a few days in my eight track studio – starting on Christmas Eve after eight weeks in Strangeways – I'd come up with 'Fountain' – the full thing. Most of *Golden Greats* came from home eight-track tapes taken into a top-class studio, transferred to 24-track and programmed through computers by Dave McCracken and built up from there. I was super lucky in making *Golden Greats* to come across Dave, programmer extraordinaire, and Steve 'Ninja Man' Fitzmaurice, world's top mixer and Tim Wills – top engineer. We got on so well we eventually wrote a few tunes together to make a complete LP from a ragbag of ideas I'd brought into the studio.❞ IAN (2001)

❝I wrote three of the songs in prison. One's called 'Free My Way', one's called 'So Many Soldiers' and me girl sent me a letter that said, 'Hey you ugly people, I want you to set my baby free,' and so I did that 'Set My Baby Free' tune. I was focusing on the day that I got out! I was counting days, definitely. I'd never been in prison before – and I didn't like it!**" IAN (2000)

Dolphins Were Monkeys

"Scientists will tell you that the dolphin as a warm-blooded mammal once lived on the land. The dolphin derives from a creature called the meryciad, which was a monkey-like creature that became a dolphin ultimately. And the scientists say that dolphins went back into the sea. Was it a conscious decision? We know that they've got brains, we know they've got their own language, quite closely linked to human beings, and to monkeys. So the dolphins were monkeys scientifically. It's a known fact.**" IAN (2000)**

"A number 5 hit with virtually no radio play. Nuff said." IAN (2002)

POST ROSES

Golden Gaze

❝An initial idea from Simon Wolstencroft was picked up by myself, then Tim the engineer, then Dave my programmer, then Mike Bennett, a producer and friend of Simon's. It became 'Golden Gaze'. A true team effort, proving five heads are better than one!❞

IAN (2002)

Music Of The Spheres LP

❝They're always going on about how I can't sing, but if I can't sing, how come I've got a record straight in at number 3 in the music charts? If you can't sing, you wouldn't get a record deal, would you? I must have something going on or people wouldn't keep buying my records. I mean, I'm not in magazines all the time, I hardly ever do promotion, I've never been on MTV.❞ **IAN (2002)**

Be There (UNKLE)

❝I did the UNKLE thing and it was the first time I've heard myself without guitars. John's one of the greatest guitarists of his generation, so is Aziz. I feel like I've worked with the best so I'd like to move away and do other things now. I feel like I've done the guitar backing. What ever instrument, I'm up for it. Except the bagpipes.❞ **IAN (2000)**

Ian's Stay In Prison

❝They jailed me for threatening behaviour on an aircraft. They said that I threatened to cut a stewardess's hands off. But I don't know what I was gonna do with me plastic fork and me plastic knife! I didn't swear at the stewardess. The captain of the aircraft was a part-time judge, so I deny all allegations that they made. But they did need a public figure. Someone to be seen to pay for the air

rage laws that they brought on and chose me. They gave me four months in prison, which was served in Strangeways Prison in Manchester. **99**

IAN (2000)

66 I got the same as Gary Glitter. I was sent away for words I'm supposed to have said, and I didn't even say the words they put me away for. He had 4,500 images of kids – and me and him get the same sentence. **99** IAN (2002)

66 First day in Strangeways, the governor says to me, 'You shouldn't be here, but you're my problem now. Are you writing songs? I've got a 19-year-old son who loves your *Unfinished Monkey Business*. Get grafting. Get him a pen.' **99** **IAN (2000)**

66 If they'd told me I'd done six months, I would have believed them. A weekend feels like a fortnight. I'd always wondered what the inside of Strangeways looked like, but maybe I should never have wondered. I know what real hunger's like now, 60 days with my belly hurting! The guys in there really looked after me too. They'd give me an apple or a newspaper, they were all like, 'What are you doing in here? You're not a criminal.' **99**

IAN (2002)

POST ROSES **99**

"I turned Muslim in jail too. It was the only way I could keep alive, food-wise. It was all dog-food pies, so I went Muslim and I got lentils, chickpeas, rice and chicken curry on Friday. They told me half of Manchester's Muslims [are] in Kirkham nick. It's the only way you can be guaranteed chicken!" IAN (2000)

"Them screws in Strangeways are like dogs, so it was tricky, because you have to keep your mouth shut and they tell you you're a knob and try and get you to respond, and you can't respond because that's what they want." IAN (2002)

"The last day when they let me out, the lads were running up and down hugging me, saying, 'Go make a million. Go sing your heart out.' The love that they were giving me was unbelievable. I was choked. It was as up there as Spike Island, definitely." IAN (2000)

"There's a lot to be said for going inside. I came out of there leaner and fitter than I've ever been. When I went in I was doing 30 press-ups and 50 sit-ups. Within six weeks I was doing 500 sit-ups and 400 press-ups, 'cos you've got the metal bed with the shape to put your feet in. I came out with a flippin' 19-pack."

IAN (2000)

"I want it to have literary worth, but I want it to be really funny as well. I've got loads of funny stories in there. I'm gonna do a chapter about The Stone Roses. I'm gonna do a chapter on the music business and I'm gonna do a chapter on 1999 and contrast it with what it was like in prison at the end of 1998."

IAN ON HIS PROJECTED BOOK (2000)

"I went into prison with no respect for authority and came out with even less. It's done one thing for me, though. I used to be known as the singer from The Stone Roses. Now I'm Ian Brown."

IAN (2000)

POST ROSES

JOHN SQUIRE
The Seahorses

❝The president phoned me up and said, 'You're still on Geffen if you want to be' and I said 'Alright'. They gave us five years and all the money we wanted to make a record – that kind of support is not to be sniffed at.❞ JOHN (1997)

❝I left the Roses at about 5 o'clock and I found my first member for the new band by about nine. It felt fated. I was toying with the name The Seahorses and after the gig, we went to a pizza restaurant and there was a five-foot fibreglass seahorse at the bottom of the stairs. JOHN (1997)

❝... now I see the Roses as something that led up to The Seahorses. No regrets now.❞ JOHN (1997)

❝It's a fresh start and I'm enjoying it much more. Everything's happening so much faster than it ever did with the Roses. There's no committee, no ego war. It's just like, 'Here's the job, let's do it. Right, what's next?'❞ JOHN (1997)

THE SEAHORSES

❝I've had a bite. I want the rest of the cake.❞ JOHN (1997)

❝I still see myself as the guitar player in the group, not their guru. I did initially see myself as the sole writer. But the songs I heard changed my mind. Chris's songs seem to flow more than mine. All of his would stand up with just an acoustic accompaniment, mine would fall to pieces.❞

JOHN (1997)

"Events kept reaffirming that it might be a good band name. I'd spot something in the *National Geographic* or on TV. The dream dictionary says the seahorse is a symbol for travel and adventure, which seemed very apt for a new band. So I took the seahorse in the restaurant as a sign – that clinched it." JOHN (1997)

"I was terrified at the first soundcheck, because it sounded appalling but the gig was pretty good. And the second gig [Rico's, Greenock] was *phenomenal*. I think the band needed to see for themselves what I saw in them."

JOHN (1997)

"Some people think I was planning all this for a long time. That's not true. There's only one song on *Do It Yourself*, 'Standing On Your Head' that was completed before I left The Stone Roses. But I didn't write it with the intention of it being the start of a secret store of songs that I could use for any, um, solo project. It was just something I held back from *Second Coming* because I felt we had enough to work on at that time. Things were going so slowly I just didn't want to add another song to the pot. But, looking back, it does seem strange that The Seahorses came together so quickly." JOHN (1997)

"I'm not a despot, not at all. You see, I think it's all right that the author of any song has the last word, and that's true for Chris [Helme, vocalist]; he has the veto on what I play on his songs, and if he felt something was inappropriate I'd change it. I don't want to be deemed a tyrant, it would be to the detriment of the band – which is what we are." JOHN (1997)

POST ROSES

❝The amount of attention we've had is ridiculous, considering the lifespan of the group; we've only been together since November. All that we've done together is make an album, so it's not surprising that the emphasis is on the music at the moment. But that's all right, it's not limiting. I don't mind being limited to Top 5 singles.❞

JOHN (1997)

❝There was a band that was ready to gig and record an album. Three of them have gone on to form The Shining.❞ JOHN (2003)

❝Tony Visconti was one of a list of producers suggested by Geffen because they asked me if I had anyone in mind and I didn't. Of all the records I listened to, Rick Rubin and Tony's names sounded best.❞ **JOHN (1997)**

❝Tony [Visconti] was one of Geffen's suggestions. I actually wanted to get Steve Albini but I was told they couldn't track him down.❞

JOHN (1997)

❝After getting over the taboo of listening to long-haired, flared-trouser musicians – the very people punk slagged off – I actually appreciated how much punk musicians had taken from before. You can hear elements of the Pistols in the first two Zeppelin albums, to be honest.❞ **JOHN (1997)**

"The drummer and the bassist walked out and the singer persuaded them to come back. But, I decided, if they were going to be that flaky, I didn't want to continue." JOHN (2003)

Love Me And Leave Me

"Yeah, I went round to his [Liam's] after the Cup Final last year. We wrote this song together and I changed the lyrics a bit, but it's basically the same song. Talking about supergroups, I would have started a group with Liam. But he's a bit busy, obviously. I'm sure we'll write more songs together, though."

JOHN ON THE SONG HE CO-WROTE WITH LIAM GALLAGHER (1997)

Do It Yourself LP

Second Coming sounded so dense because it was completely overworked. And this one was the complete antithesis of that, it felt more like the first album than the first Roses did. There was no labouring." JOHN (1997)

"I listen to this record and the Roses and I prefer this. It's a simpler record, but I think it's a better one. *Second Coming* is too long. I can't listen to more than 45 minutes in one sitting. And I like this record 'cos it's got three of Chris's songs on. That makes it more interesting for me." JOHN (1997)

"There was a philosophy with *Do It Yourself* of taking it back to basics. I didn't want this record to sound like a continuation of the Roses, a sequel to *Second Coming*. I wanted it to sound like a debut album, so we contrived to capture the live sound and not spend too much time slicing it up and layering. I think that's something we'll do next time..." JOHN (1997)

POST ROSES

JOHN SQUIRE SOLO

Time Changes Everything

"It was the first time since the Roses that I didn't have a plan. But I eventually decided that I'd had enough of trying to break in singers and have my ideas refracted through somebody else." JOHN (2002)

"I was lazy really. I find it hard looking for musicians, looking for singers particularly. I spent a lot of time looking for the vocalist I worked with after The Seahorses and I lived with the guy three or four nights a week. He practically moved into my house and we worked intensively on his voice and on the songs, and it all fell apart after about a year and I couldn't face the prospect of going through all that again. So short of quitting music all together, my options were narrowed to taking centre stage myself." JOHN (2003)

"The first songs were recorded with just a drum machine and acoustic, so I thought it was just going to be something like that: folksy with a few drum loops spun in. I remember thinking *Mellow Gold* by Beck was somewhere I could probably take it." JOHN (2002)

"It was a gradual thing. I made the decision that I was going to sing every day, and see how good it would get. The real test I was going to apply to myself was getting Simon [Jones – ex-Verve bassist] to record something. And if I could bear to listen to the results, I'd carry on. It was daunting just to sing to another person. I've got a lot more respect for the people I've worked with in the past now, probably than I had at the time. It's so much more physical than playing the guitar. I understand why singers don't want to sing all day." JOHN FINDS HIS VOICE (2002)

"I was actually quite surprised. I'm well aware of people like John Lennon who said they hated the sound of their own vocals, and doing anything they can to mask them. I was steeling myself for that experience, which was obviously weird, but I don't mind it at all." JOHN (2002)

POST ROSES

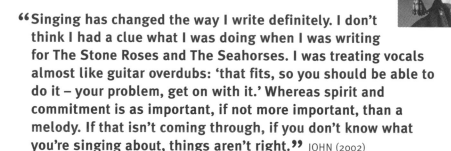

"Singing has changed the way I write definitely. I don't think I had a clue what I was doing when I was writing for The Stone Roses and The Seahorses. I was treating vocals almost like guitar overdubs: 'that fits, so you should be able to do it – your problem, get on with it.' Whereas spirit and commitment is as important, if not more important, than a melody. If that isn't coming through, if you don't know what you're singing about, things aren't right." JOHN (2002)

"It was all about the vocal. When we started, I didn't know whether I could finish the album or not. Next time around, I'd like to bring in more of the guitar playing into the songwriting process... get the riffs going again." **JOHN (2003)**

"I think I spent too long trying to be a better guitar player. I should have spent more time writing songs. I would have written better songs if I'd put the effort into the rudiments of singing. It's far too masturbatory, sitting there with a guitar in your thirties." JOHN (2002)

"I'd like next, when I've got a stronger voice to write with an electric guitar, and not focus so much on the vocal." **JOHN (2003)**

15 Days

"It was spewed out. After the first couple of lines it was like taking my finger out of a dam. I've maybe been writing it subliminally for the last seven years." **JOHN (2002)**

"I enjoyed those times a lot. I miss it still. But I don't want to go back. I wrote the lyrics as I was playing the guitar. It felt good to sing. I don't know how it scans as poetry. And I still don't know how it makes me feel: a strange combination of satisfaction with the song and the performance and, at the same time, remembering what went on. I like the way it tumbles along. I don't think I'd have given something so naked to a third person."

JOHN ON THE SONG FROM HIS SOLO ALBUM THAT TOOK ITS TITLE AND
FIRST LINE FROM 'FOOLS GOLD' (2002)

MANI

Primal Scream

"We've got a lot in common. I astound the Scream with my energy, my capacity to party. It's just the way I am. I love life, man. You'd never see me doing a Kurt Cobain. What's great with the Scream is, and it might sound corny, but it's like being part of a family again. It always was with The Stone Roses, we were so tight. And it's the same in the Scream.

"I always knew it was gonna work. Under the Bosman Rule, Mounfield is free to move now. And it's the best move I could've made. I'm nudging Gillespie out of the middle, man, and having it for myself." MANI (1999)

POST ROSES

❝I don't know whether you'd call it luck. You have to create your own luck. But there is an element of right place, right time, right style and right talent for what you're doing. It feels good. I got a good education with the Roses boys, learnt a lot of tricks – especially from Reni – and now I'm getting the chance to put it into practice with the Scream.❞ MANI (2000)

Xtrmntr

❝We're in a bit of murky water at the minute with this publishing company who are trying to screw us for another LP when we've fulfilled the thing with them. So once again, it's this court monkey business that follows Gary Mounfield about, man. It's put the brakes on it for a bit. We've got songs but we're just a bit reluctant to record them just in case this label says we want them now. We wanna get a new deal and then it's a buzz for us. What we have written is staggering. It's punk, rock, dub, The Who, The Stooges on *Raw Power*, it's everything. It's just a step on from *Vanishing Point* again. It's a lot more experimental as well. That's what I like about it. It's dangerous.❞ **MANI (1999)**

❝We were always interested in dance music. Whether it was Northern soul or rock'n'roll, we've always had that about us in both bands. So I don't think it's a surprise that you hear Mr Brown coming out sounding funky as fuck or Primal Scream sounding the same. We've all come out of the house movement. We were all like-minded in a certain way, y'know, giving everyone a new vibe and a new way of thinking about things.❞ MANI (2000)

❝I feel really upbeat and positive about it. We've just got a feeling that it's time for Primal Scream at the moment. There is so much shit about that we feel it's time for something decent... hopefully we're not too exotic for mass consumption. We don't sound like anything else and we may be a little bit twisted and a little bit warped in our way but I really hope that it really does get on it, because it's about time.❞ **MANI (2000)**

Swastika Eyes

66Yeah, it's socially aware of what's going on. It's a good
commentary on what Bobby [Gillespie] sees around him. It's the
Americanisation of the planet with the WTO and the International
Monetary Fund, NATO and all that.99 **MANI (2000)**

The Complete Stone Roses Tribute Band

66It's pretty weird but I'm buzzing to see it because I've never seen
The Stone Roses if you see what I mean. I first heard about Stone
Roses tribute bands when the Scream played the SFX and I saw a
poster for The Stone Roses and I thought, 'I'd love to turn up at
that and see their faces.' But apparently these guys tonight are

good. Apparently they can play the songs really well, probably better than us at our most E'd when we couldn't hit a note. They gotta be better than that, man. I just love being out of the house. All I'd be doing now is sitting watching *Casualty*, waiting for *Match Of The Day*, having a few fat spliffs. Listen, any chance I get to come 'ere mate, I'm having it. Last weekend we did Scotland and this weekend over here. More power to the Gaels, man. **"**

MANI, DUBLIN, MEAN FIDDLER (1999)

"Oh, I'd love to play with the Jimi Hendrix Experience tribute band. I'd be Noel Redding, obviously. I've been working on Ian Brown's guitarist Aziz Ibrahim's solo album and he's done a few tunes with Noel so I think I'm probably gonna get to meet him. Apparently, he's a right old arsehole." MANI (1999)

DJ-ing

"I just kinda fell into it. Smithy (Phil Smith) who lives in me house has been travelling as DJ with Oasis, so I just dug me vinyl out and said, 'I'm doin' a bit of that an' all.' I enjoy it because I'm a music lover and I've got some proper, obscure funky soul grooves, lots of rare grooves and shit. That's what I'll be playing, some proper good funk.**"** **MANI (1999)**

"Yeah, Fat Boy Slim getting ten grand for a gig on New Year's Eve. That's bonkers. Whoever the promoters of these gigs are, I'm bang up for it, man. And I'm a fuckin' legend. But it's another interpretation of other people's music. I suppose it's an art form in itself. I saw those guys from Bass Odyssey last night. When they were getting the scratching going I was well impressed. I need to get some decks in me house and learn how to do that shit. It'll be cool. There's nothing I can't do. I could be the fuckin' Primate of Ireland if I wanted." MANI (1999)

POST ROSES

Loose Talk (Fans & Friends)

"The [Happy] Mondays and Stone Roses have the same influences, 'cos we've been to the same clubs. Blues nights, reggae nights, house nights, a bit of Parliament, a bit of Funkadelic... we're all takin' it from the same record collections, just doin' it up different. They're the only other group we can just sit down and have a drink with." **IAN (1990)**

"The only rivalry between us and the Roses is over clothes. There's always been a bit of a race on to see who's got the best flashiest clothes and what part of the world these clothes come from. 'Cos we're both flash coonts, y'know what I mean?"

SHAUN RYDER, HAPPY MONDAYS (1990)

"They're dead brilliant, Stone Roses. They're more tuneful than us but we're a top band too. I can call 'em mates. Ian! Fookin' Mani! Remi! [*sic*] Friends, y'know what I mean? And particularly fookin' Cressa, man! We taught him everythin' he fookin' knows!"

SHAUN RYDER, HAPPY MONDAYS (1990)

"In Britain, it's about your style or where you come from, your haircut, whether you like The Stone Roses or whether you think such-a-body is shit." CLINT BOON, INSPIRAL CARPETS (1991)

SICE (BOO RADLEYS), IAN BROWN,
ROBBIE MADDIX AND NOEL GALLAGHER

LOOSE TALK

"A great band is a great band and they [the Roses] haven't waylaid themselves in the way that my lot – the Mondays – did." **HACIENDA/FACTORY RECORDS BOSS ANTHONY WILSON (1994)**

"**We love Oasis... we're their dads!**" MANI (1994)

"It was the first gig I ever went to. And Ian Brown came on and he was giving it the vibe and all that..." **LIAM GALLAGHER (1994)**

TONY WILSON

"**This guy [Liam] didn't know what the fuck he was going on about until The Stone Roses, and he could totally identify with Ian Brown. And I went 'Now d'you know what I've been talking about for the past 10 years?'**" NOEL GALLAGHER (1994)

"I can't explain it but when I saw The Stone Roses on stage, it did something to me. They were real people, doing it from the heart and they just treated everything about themselves dead special, which is right." **LIAM GALLAGHER (1994)**

LIAM GALLAGHER

❝Their (*Second Coming*) album's better than all the rest that's
around, apart from us. It's alright, but five years is a long time,
y'know? And even though it's different, I don't think they're
writing songs any more. It's a shame, 'cos that's what they were
good at. I loved them first time around, I was a big fan. But we're
better than them nowadays; and as a songwriter, our kid pees
all over John Squire.❞ LIAM GALLAGHER (1995)

❝Jarvis Cocker said recently that, without Ian Brown, The Stone
Roses would have become a heavy metal band. I know exactly
where he's coming from.❞ IAN (2000)

❝The last great British band was The Stone Roses. There hasn't
been a band to touch them since. It's like me and Nick Kent with
Noel Gallagher and John Squire – the other one's cleaned up
while the talented one's scraping a living, which hardly seems
very fair!❞ TONY PARSONS (2001)

❝The gig they played in the village marquee after they cancelled
their 1995 Glastonbury appearance was one of the best I've ever
seen.❞ EMILY EAVIS, GLASTONBURY CO-ORGANISER (2003)

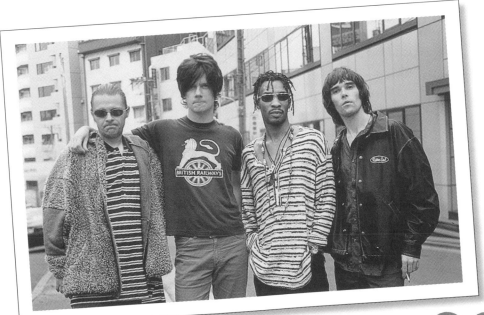

LOOSE TALK ❞❞

The Resurrection

"I went, 'No fucking way, man, it's Ian Brown.' And we were just like, we embraced and even though we don't see each other in like a year, it's like we met yesterday. I kind of miss working with the guy. If we wrote a song that merited an excellent vocal then, yeah man, Ian can do it. He's always been a funky monkey. He's working with a couple of good programmers, you know, and more of a technology-based thing. It's something he always wanted to do and I'm happy for him.**"** **MANI ON RUNNING INTO IAN IN NEW YORK (2000)**

"I'm of the belief that you should never say never. Who knows what might happen – I'd love to reform to just do the summer festivals and give all these people a chance to actually see us and see us doing it well. For me it finished in such a smelly and horrible way that I'd like to just do something to close the book once and for all and then I'd be happy." MANI (2000)

"I wouldn't hold my breath really. It'd be a nice thing to do but I don't know whether it would ever happen.**"** **MANI (2000)**

"I'm still good friends with Reni. I don't see Mani and I don't see John. I've heard a few tracks of Reni's, what I've heard's fucking knockout, yeah. He's playing guitar and singing, he's got a nice tight set up there." IAN (2000)

"You could offer me Mars and Jupiter and it still wouldn't be enough.**"** IAN (2000)

"We're the Roses, man. We don't do things like that."
IAN ON THE REPUTED £2 MILLION OFFERED TO REFORM FOR TWO FESTIVAL DATES (2000)

"I can honestly say I've thought about the band every single day since I quit. At least something, some memory every day.**"**
JOHN (2002)

"I saw John a few months back. I didn't recognise him at first. We ended up back at mine. The spliffs were out and we were drinking and just laughing about the old days. The room was full of other people, but nothing else mattered – it was me and him. I don't see enough of him, or Ian or Reni neither." MANI (2002)

"There have been times when I've sat down and thought about it and I've fucking cried. For me The Stone Roses are unfinished business. I'd love to get together one summer and go out and finish it off. Do it right. And I think the world still needs it. But at the end of the day, no music is worth losing a valued friendship for. And ultimately I value friendship more than the music. I regret some of the things that have been said. It's been blurted and it's not been meant. We really do love each other passionately. Life would be boring if there weren't problems and obstacles. I never hated any of those guys.**"** MANI (2002)

THE RESURRECTION

“I look back and I see that me and Ian had a great working relationship. We were always planning for the band and we had a definite sense of direction. And me and Reni had a great musical rapport... and Mani was the secret ingredient. It seems like yesterday to me in a lot of respects. I suppose it all spreads itself out and becomes equidistant. I don't look back at it in a kind of chronological order. It all seems to have happened at the same time, somehow.” JOHN (2002)

“It would be a tremendous emotional high. We'd need mountains of Kleenex.” **JOHN (2002)**

“I could see it happening before I died.” JOHN (2002)

“... I'm not reluctant to talk about the Roses but I can't commit to a date, having not spoken to any of the other parties involved.”
JOHN (2002)

"I don't want to do a reunion tour, because that would be putting matters to rest in the wrong way. If we were to reform, it would have to be to make a new album, and do a proper tour with new songs. I believe that will happen one day." JOHN (2002)

"It's something I could never contemplate until I find out exactly what blame Ian lays at my door." JOHN (2003)

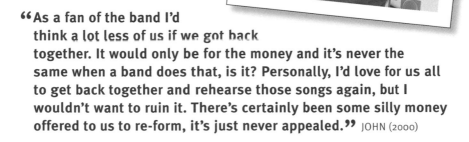

"As a fan of the band I'd think a lot less of us if we got back together. It would only be for the money and it's never the same when a band does that, is it? Personally, I'd love for us all to get back together and rehearse those songs again, but I wouldn't want to ruin it. There's certainly been some silly money offered to us to re-form, it's just never appealed." JOHN (2000)

"I don't believe in bearing grudges. But if he [Ian] stands by everything he's said then I would rather remove my liver with a teaspoon. I'm still in touch with Mani and it would be a lot easier if the rest of us could communicate. It's difficult." JOHN (2003)

"It's long overdue." JOHN ON A RECONCILIATION WITH IAN (2002)

"I don't think my solo LPs will ever make the impact The Stone Roses did. If I had a voice like Marvin Gaye I could, but I haven't. So I don't believe that I'll ever change the landscape of music like the Roses seemed to." IAN (2000)

"I can't say I miss it. I had it, I loved it and what I do now is a different thing. I'm still working with great lads, they're great players." IAN (2002)

THE RESURRECTION